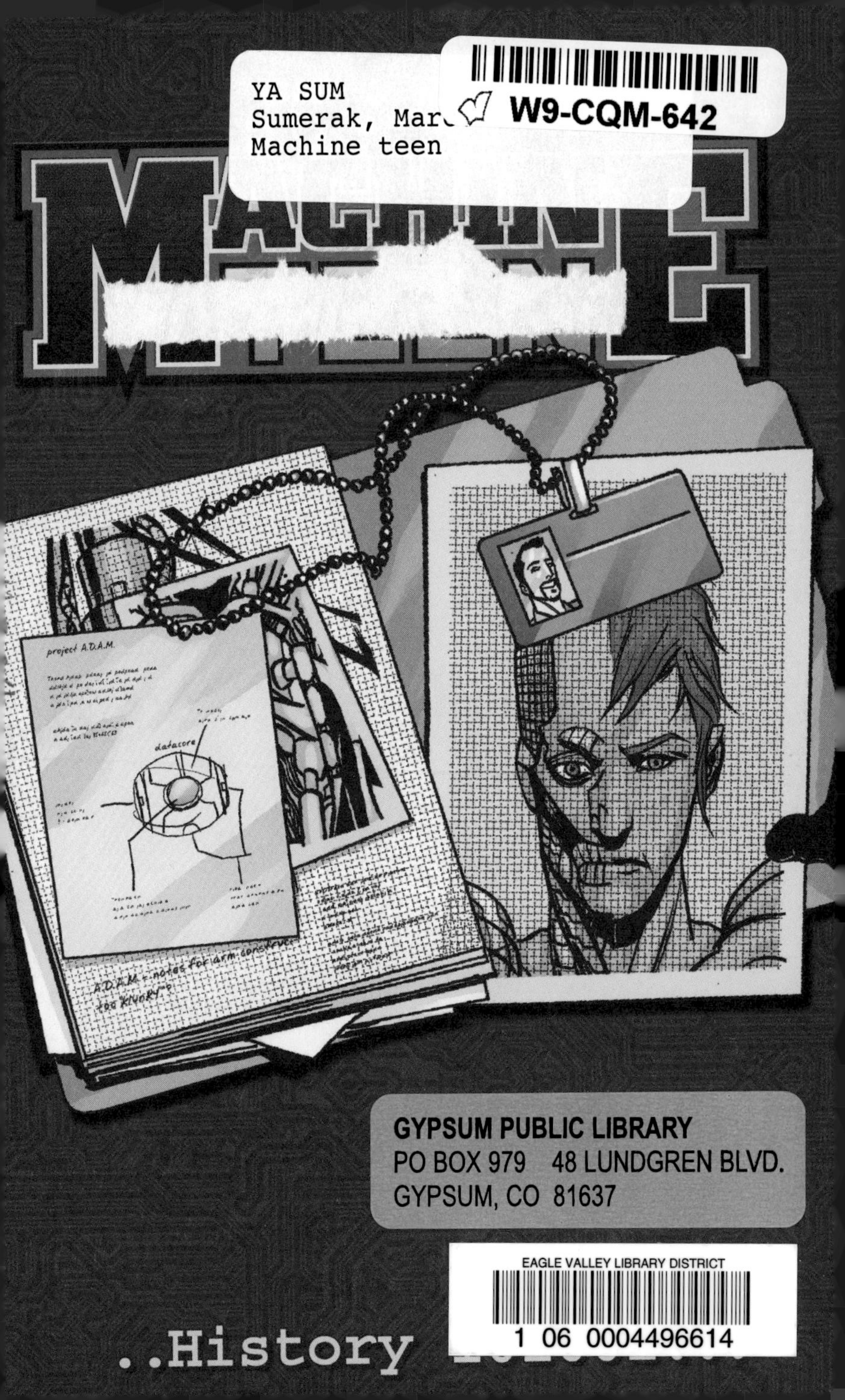
project A.D.A.M.
datacore
A.D.A.M. - notes for arm construct
too klunky

..History

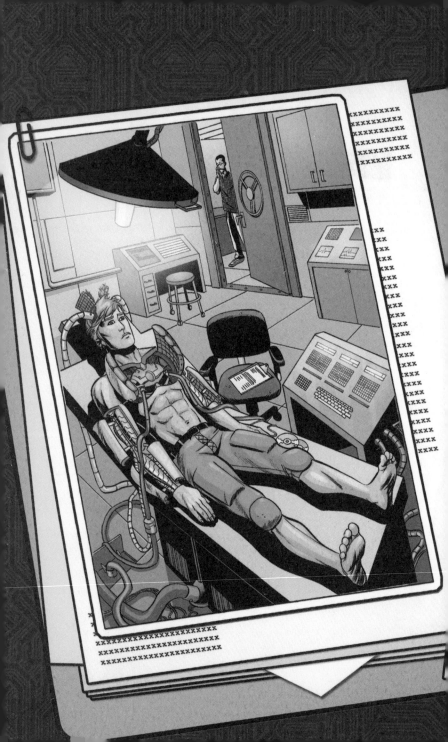

MACHINE TEEN

..History 101001...

WRITER: Marc Sumerak
ARTIST: Mike Hawthorne
INKER (ISSUES #4-5): Drew Hennessy
COLORIST: Mike Atiyeh
LETTERERS: Virtual Calligraphy's
Mike Sellers & Dave Sharpe
COVERS: James Jean & Mike Hawthorne
with Mike Atiyeh
ASSISTANT EDITOR: Nathan Cosby
EDITOR: MacKenzie Cadenhead
CONSULTING EDITOR: Mark Paniccia

MACHINE TEEN CREATED BY:
Marc Sumerak & Mike Hawthorne

COLLECTION EDITOR: Jennifer Grünwald
ASSISTANT EDITOR: Michael Short
SENIOR EDITOR, SPECIAL PROJECTS: Jeff Youngquist
DIRECTOR OF SALES: David Gabriel
BOOK DESIGNER: Carrie Beadle
CREATIVE DIRECTOR: Tom Marvelli

EDITOR IN CHIEF: Joe Quesada
PUBLISHER: Dan Buckley

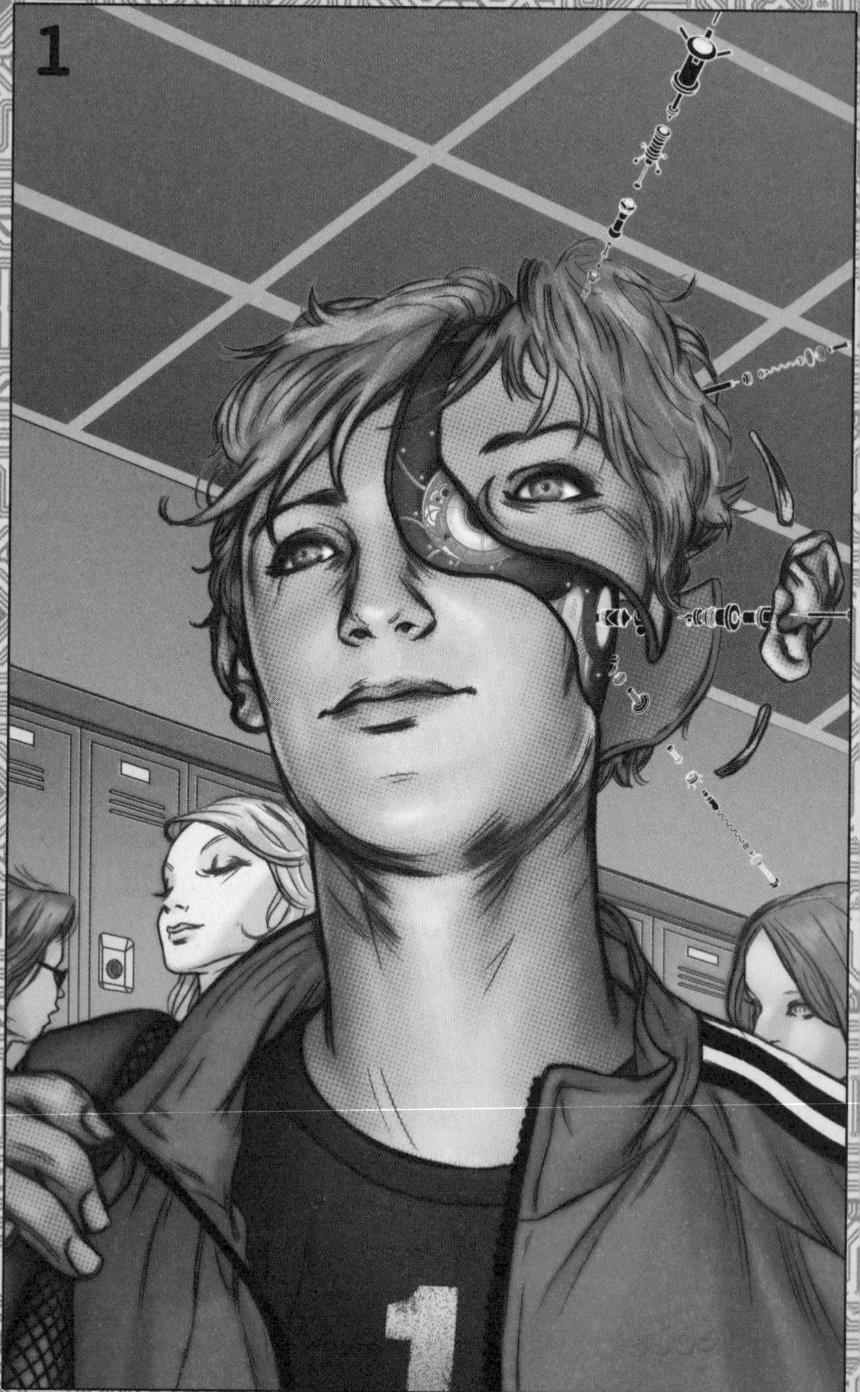
1

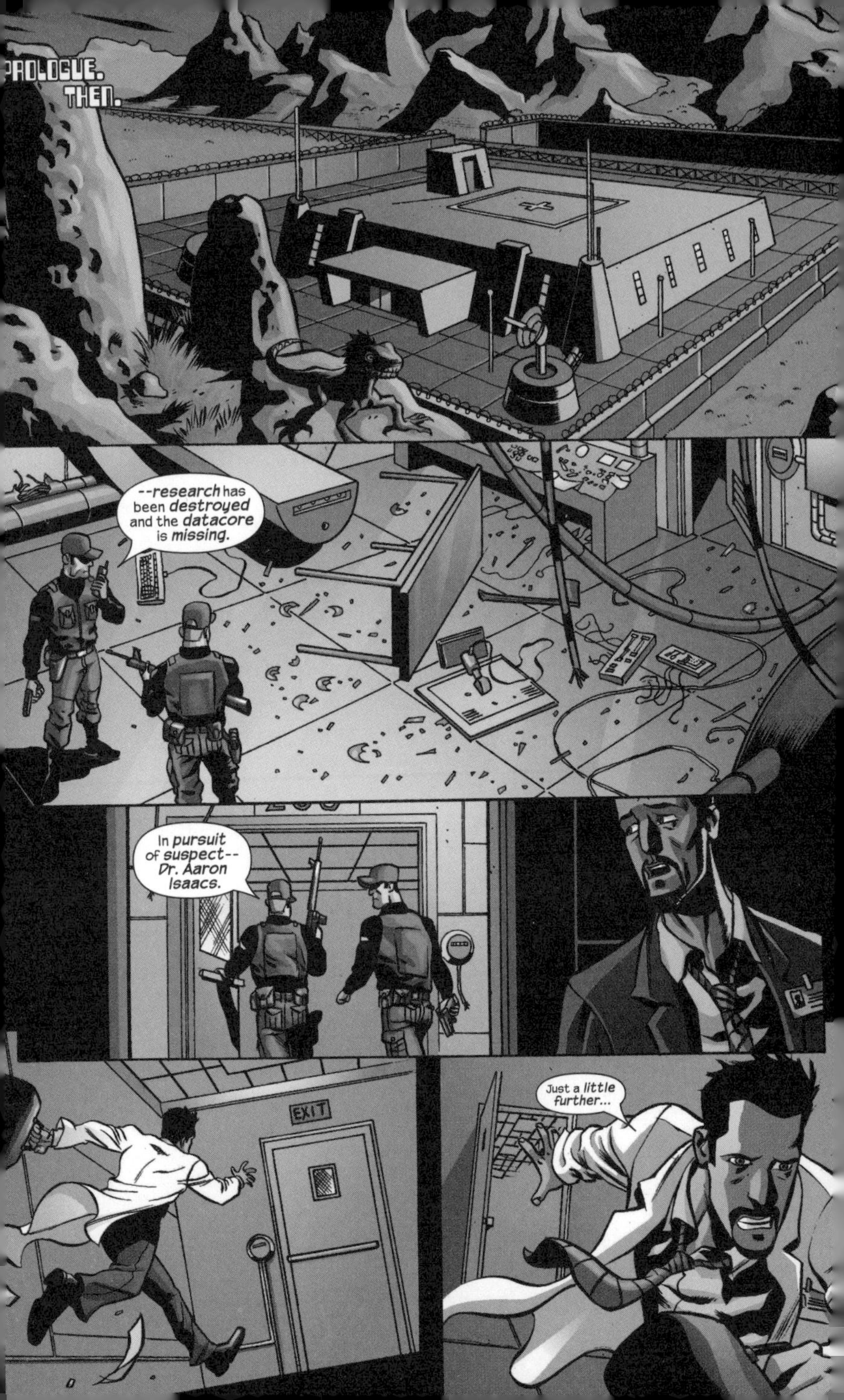
PROLOGUE.
THEN.
--research has been destroyed and the datacore is missing.
In pursuit of suspect-- Dr. Aaron Isaacs.
EXIT
Just a little further...

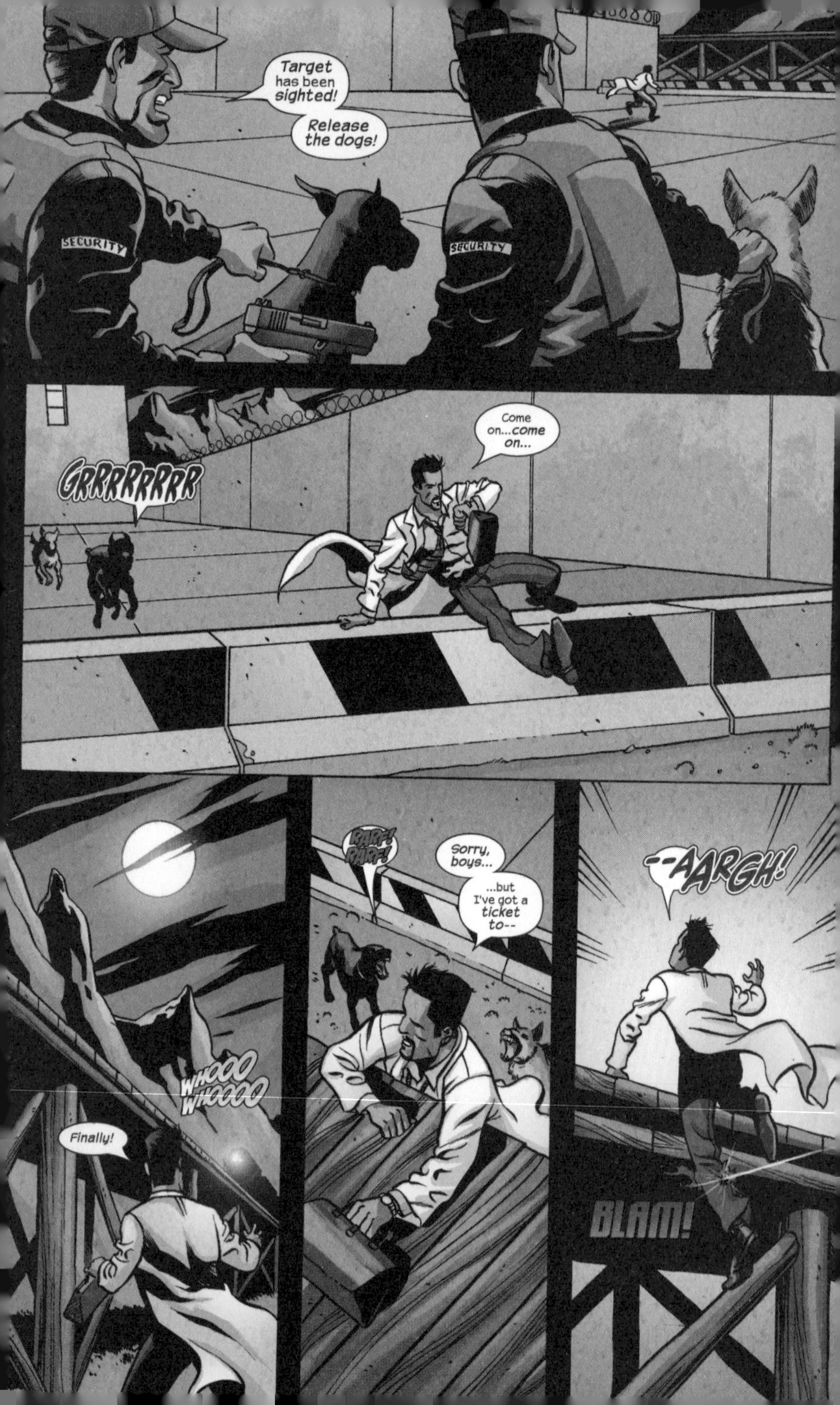
Target has been sighted!
Release the dogs!
SECURITY
SECURITY
Come on...come on...
GRRRRRRRR
WHOOO WHOOOO
Finally!
BARF! BARF!
Sorry, boys...
...but I've got a ticket to--
--AARGH!
BLAM!

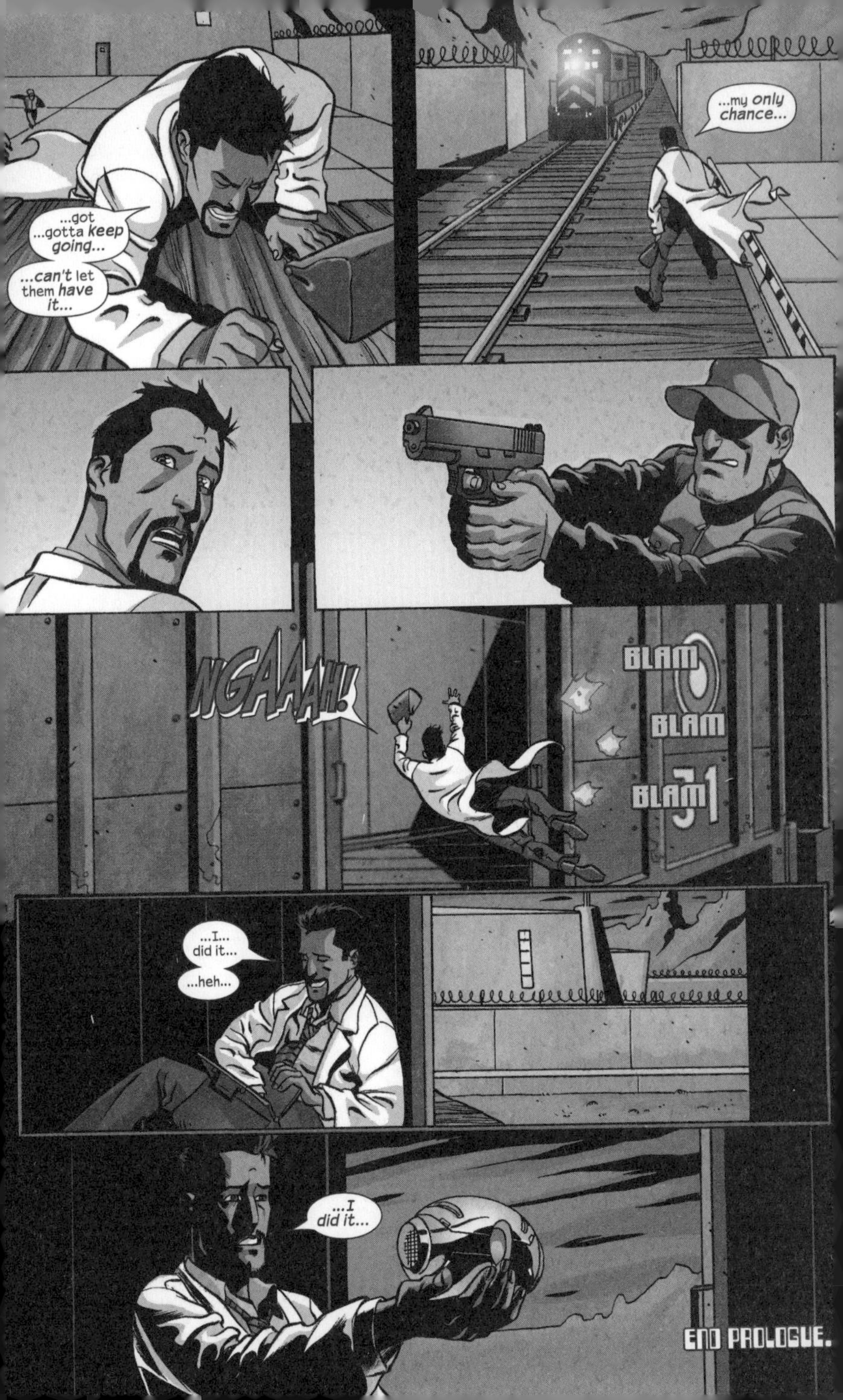
...got ...gotta keep going...
...can't let them have it...
...my only chance...
NGAAAH!
BLAM
BLAM
BLAM
31
...I... did it...
...heh...
...I did it...
END PROLOGUE.

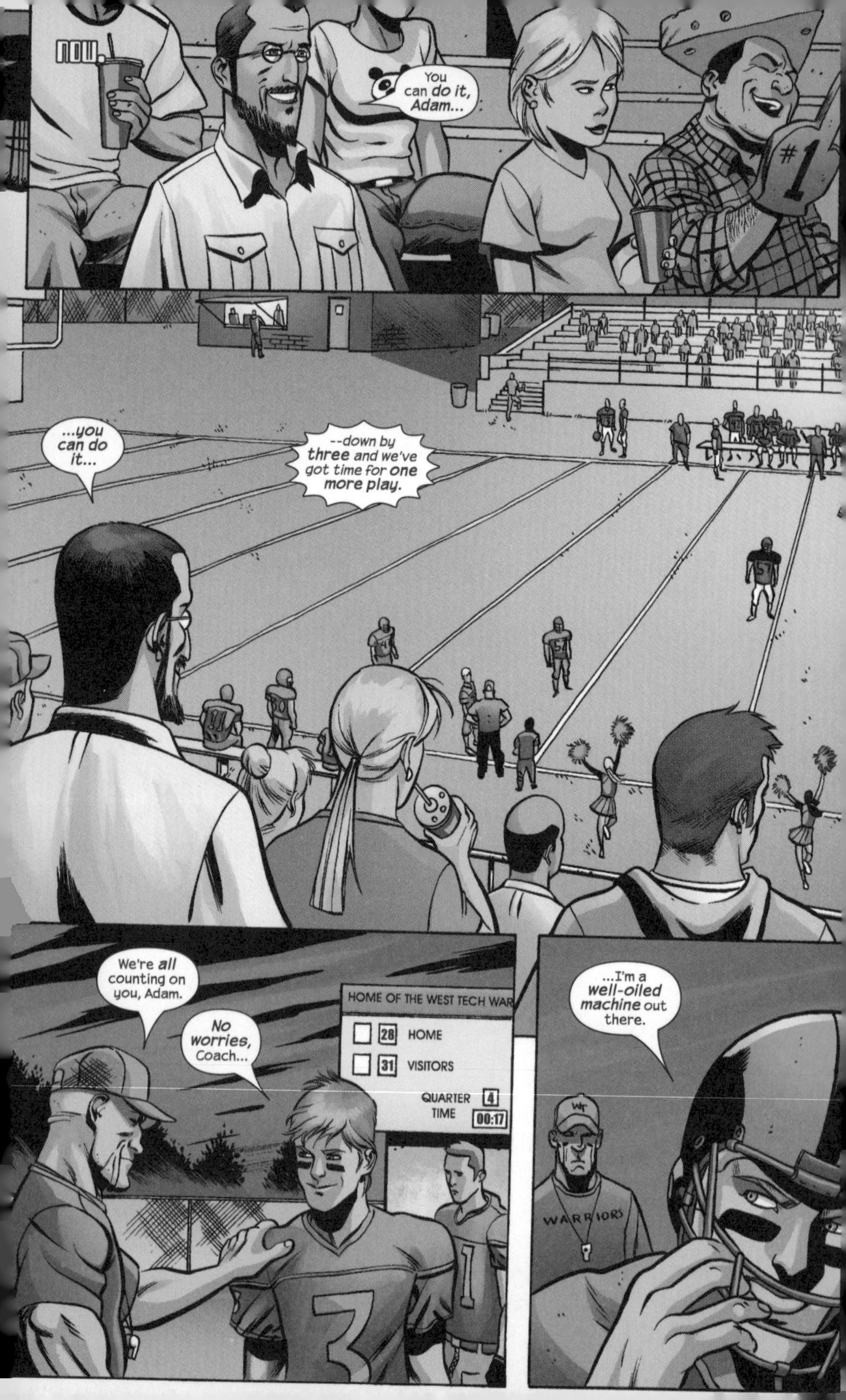
NOW...
You can do it, Adam...
...you can do it...
--down by three and we've got time for one more play.
We're all counting on you, Adam.
No worries, Coach...
HOME OF THE WEST TECH WAR
28 HOME
31 VISITORS
QUARTER 4
TIME 00:17
...I'm a well-oiled machine out there.
WARRIORS

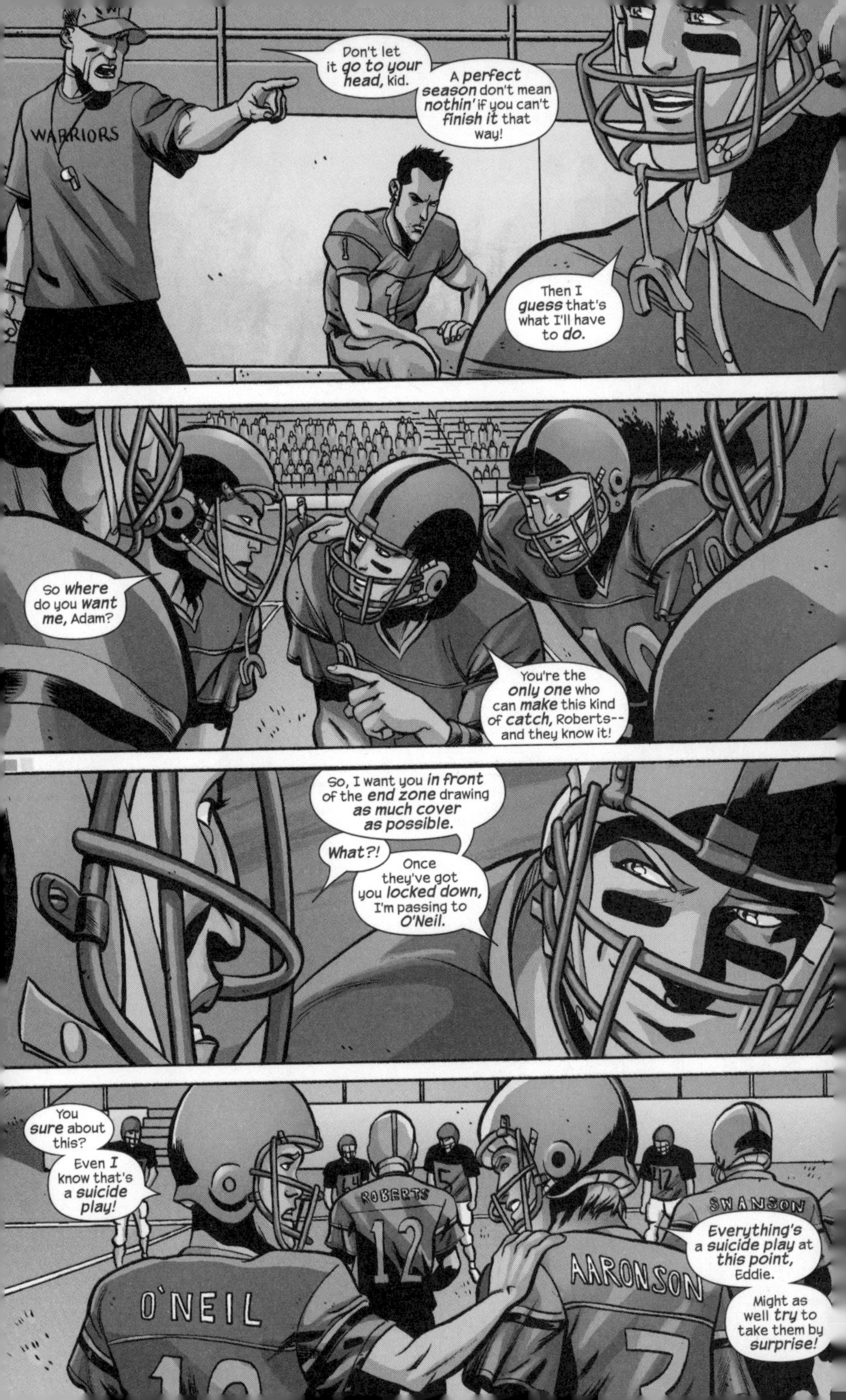
Don't let it go to your head, kid.
A perfect season don't mean nothin' if you can't finish it that way!
WARRIORS
Then I guess that's what I'll have to do.
So where do you want me, Adam?
You're the only one who can make this kind of catch, Roberts-- and they know it!
So, I want you in front of the end zone drawing as much cover as possible.
What?!
Once they've got you locked down, I'm passing to O'Neil.
You sure about this?
Even I know that's a suicide play!
ROBERTS
SWANSON
O'NEIL
AARONSON
Everything's a suicide play at this point, Eddie.
Might as well try to take them by surprise!

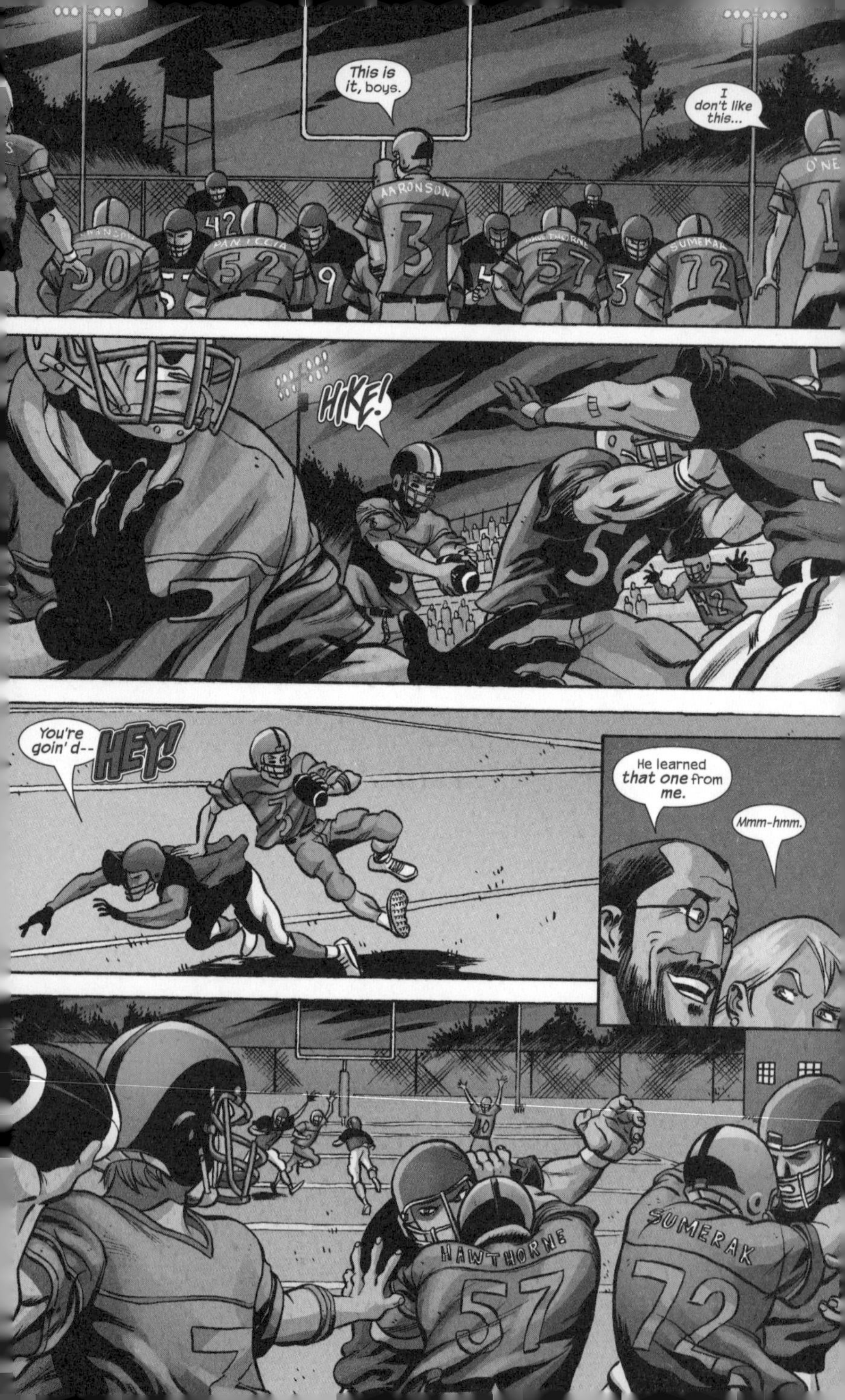
This is it, boys.
I don't like this...
AARONSON
SUMERAK
HIKE!
You're goin' d--
HEY!
He learned that one from me.
Mmm-hmm.
HAWTHORNE
SUMERAK

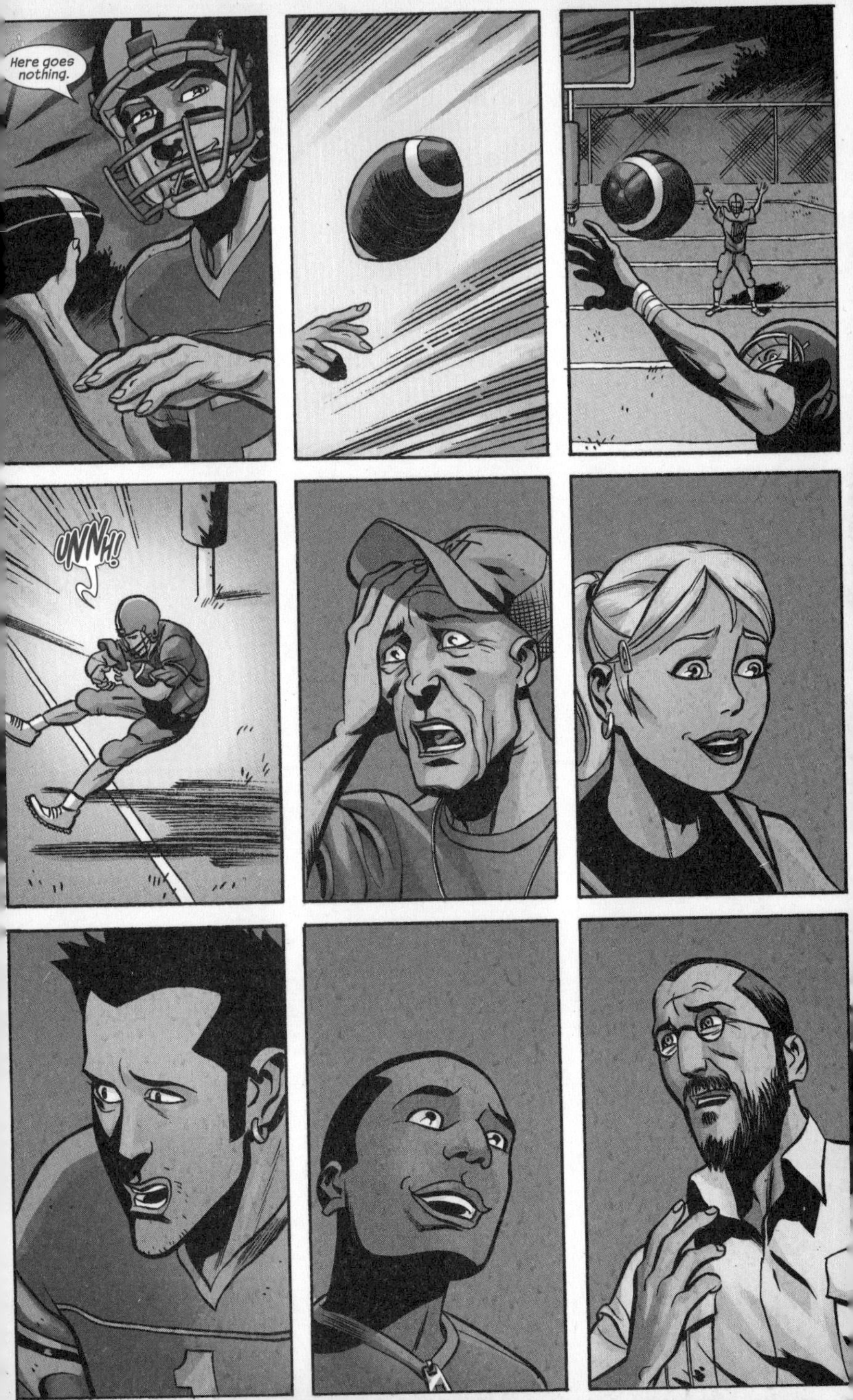
Here goes nothing.
UNNH!

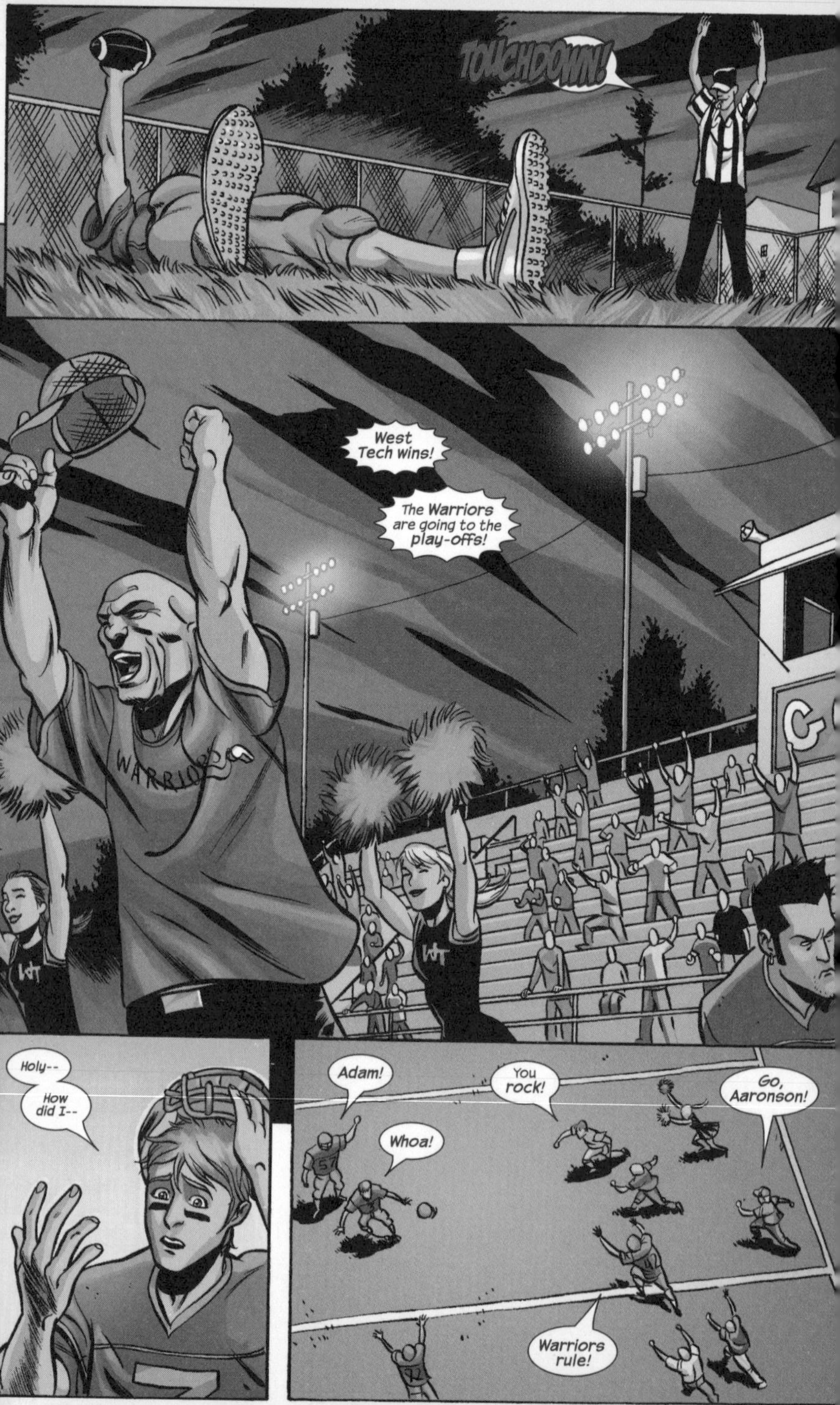
TOUCHDOWN!
West Tech wins!
The Warriors are going to the play-offs!
Holy--
How did I--
Adam!
Whoa!
You rock!
Go, Aaronson!
Warriors rule!

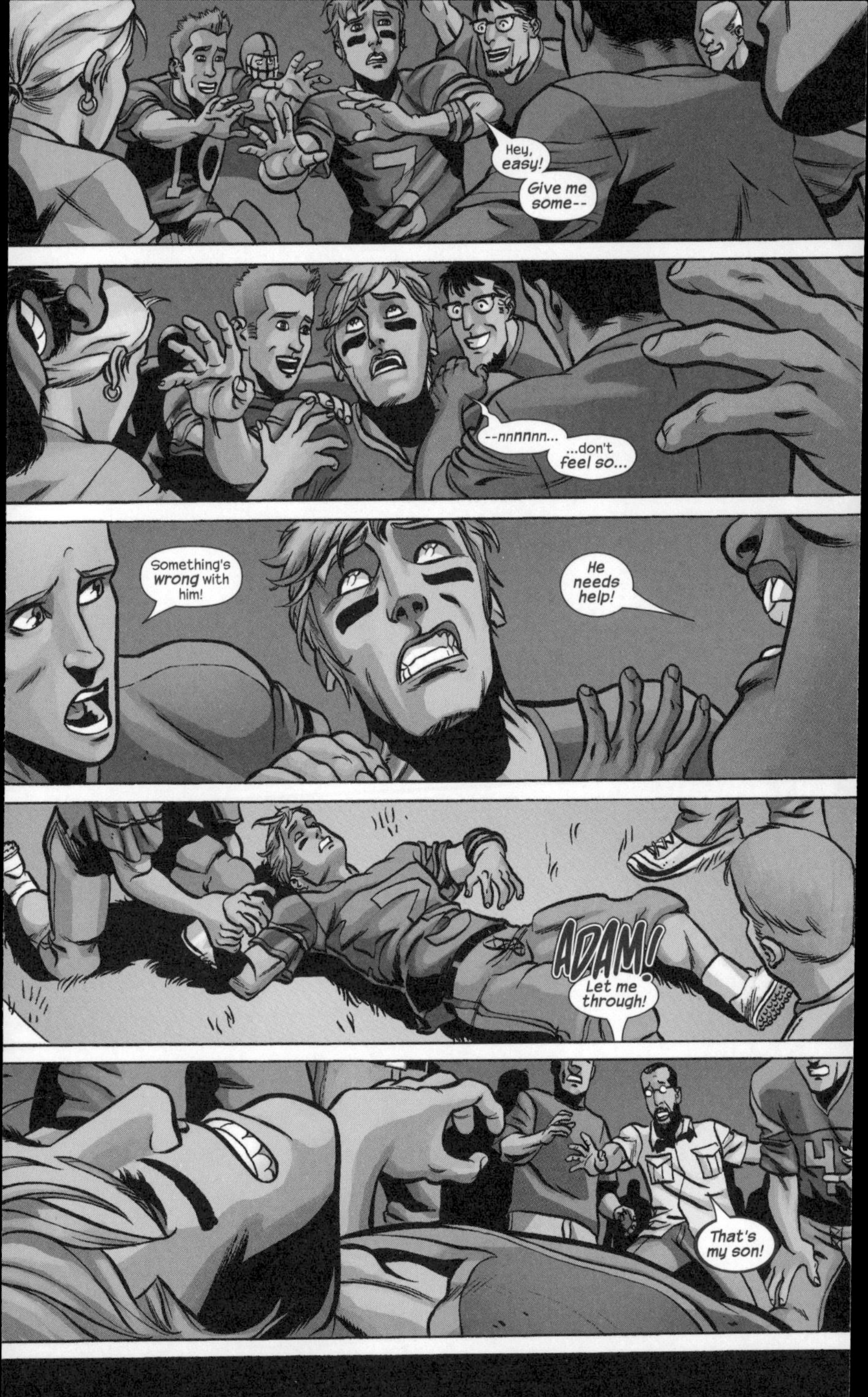
Hey, easy!
Give me some--
--nnnnnn...
...don't feel so...
Something's *wrong* with him!
He needs help!
ADAM!
Let me through!
That's my son!

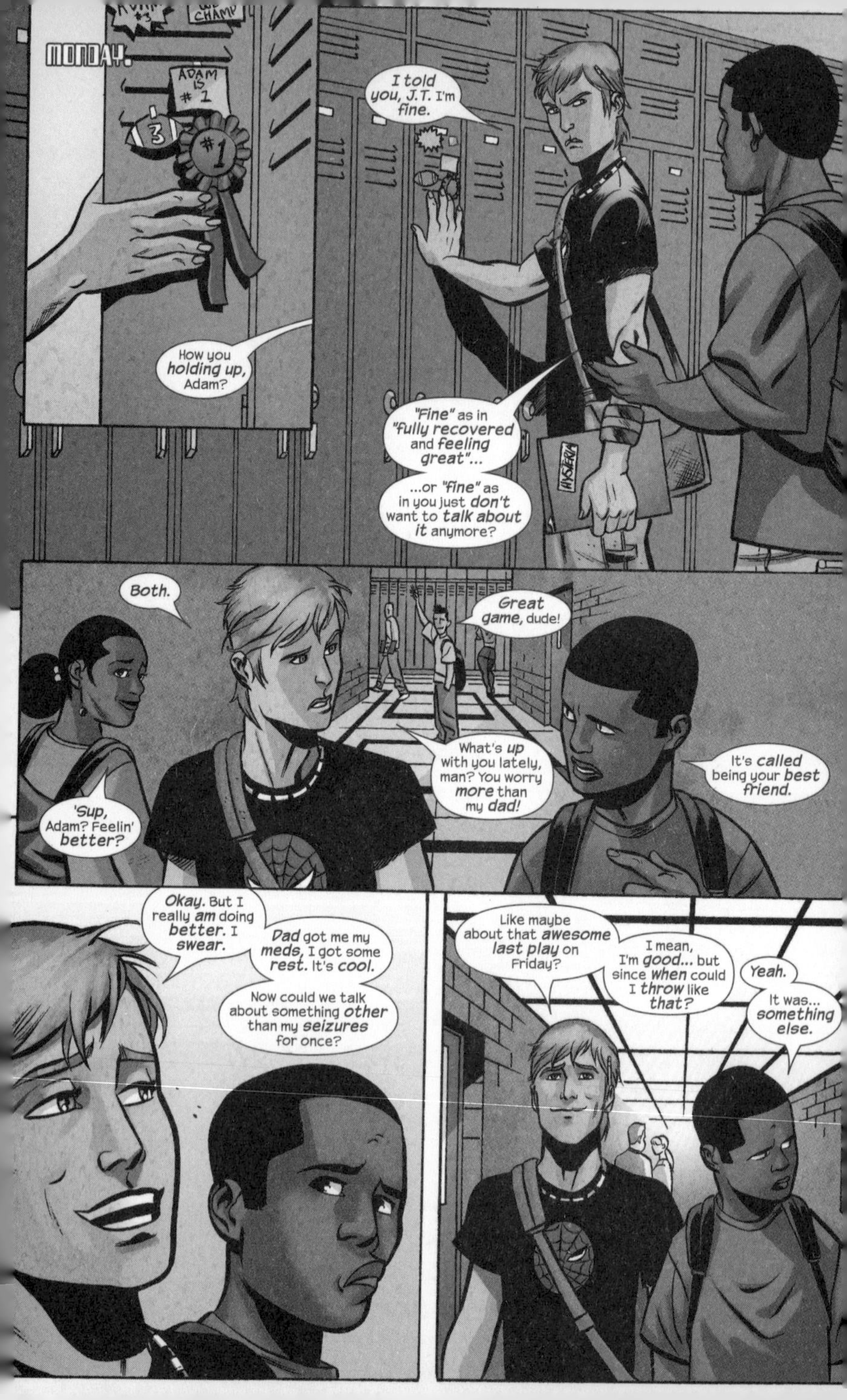
MONDAY.
ADAM IS #1
#1
3
CHAMP
I told you, J.T. I'm fine.
How you holding up, Adam?
"Fine" as in "fully recovered and feeling great"...
...or "fine" as in you just don't want to talk about it anymore?
HYSTERIA
Both.
Great game, dude!
'Sup, Adam? Feelin' better?
What's up with you lately, man? You worry more than my dad!
It's called being your best friend.
Okay. But I really am doing better. I swear.
Dad got me my meds, I got some rest. It's cool.
Now could we talk about something other than my seizures for once?
Like maybe about that awesome last play on Friday?
I mean, I'm good... but since when could I throw like that?
Yeah.
It was... something else.

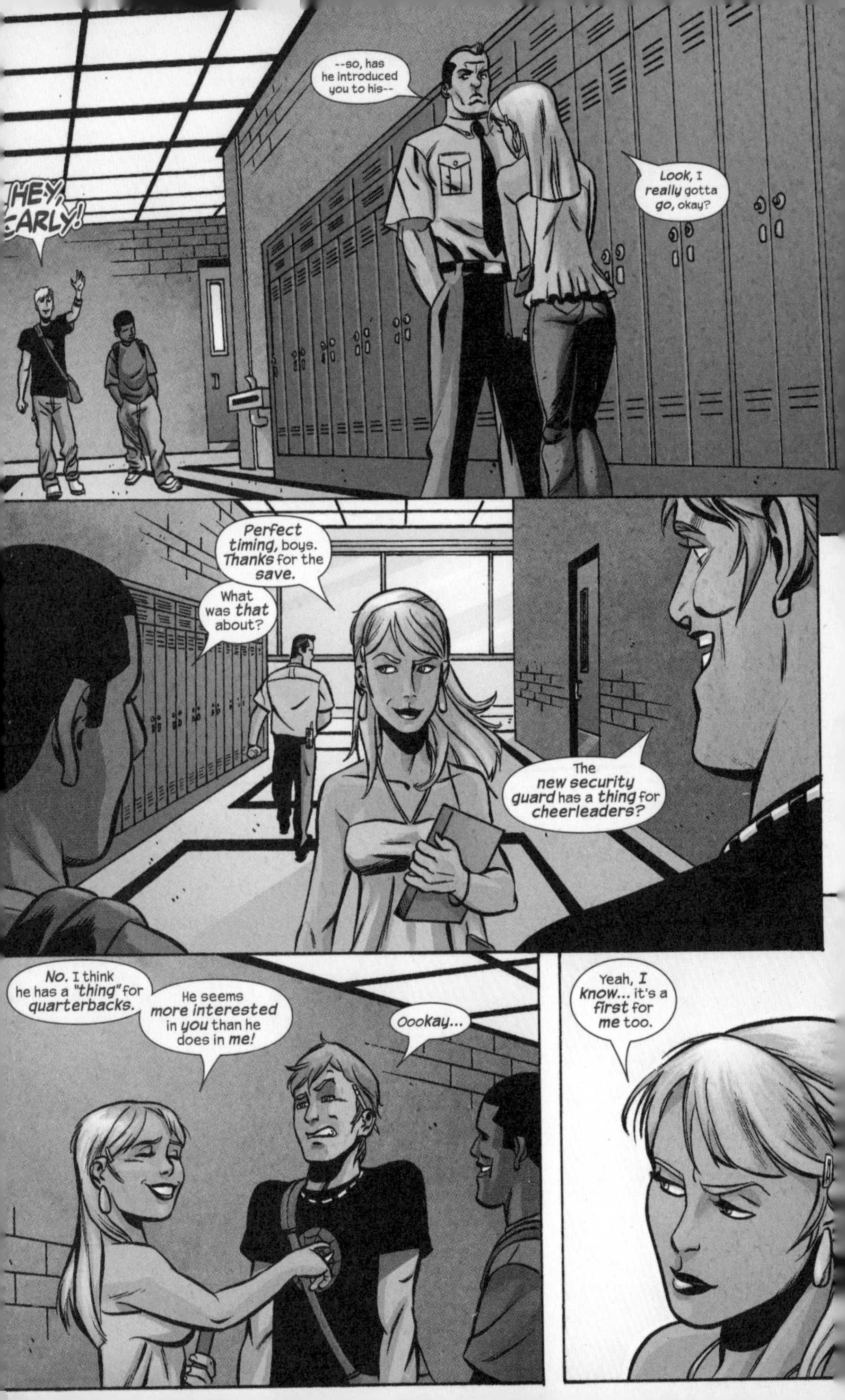

--so, has he introduced you to his--
HEY, CARLY!
Look, I really gotta go, okay?
Perfect timing, boys. Thanks for the save.
What was that about?
The new security guard has a thing for cheerleaders?
No. I think he has a "thing" for quarterbacks.
He seems more interested in you than he does in me!
Oookay...
Yeah, I know... it's a first for me too.

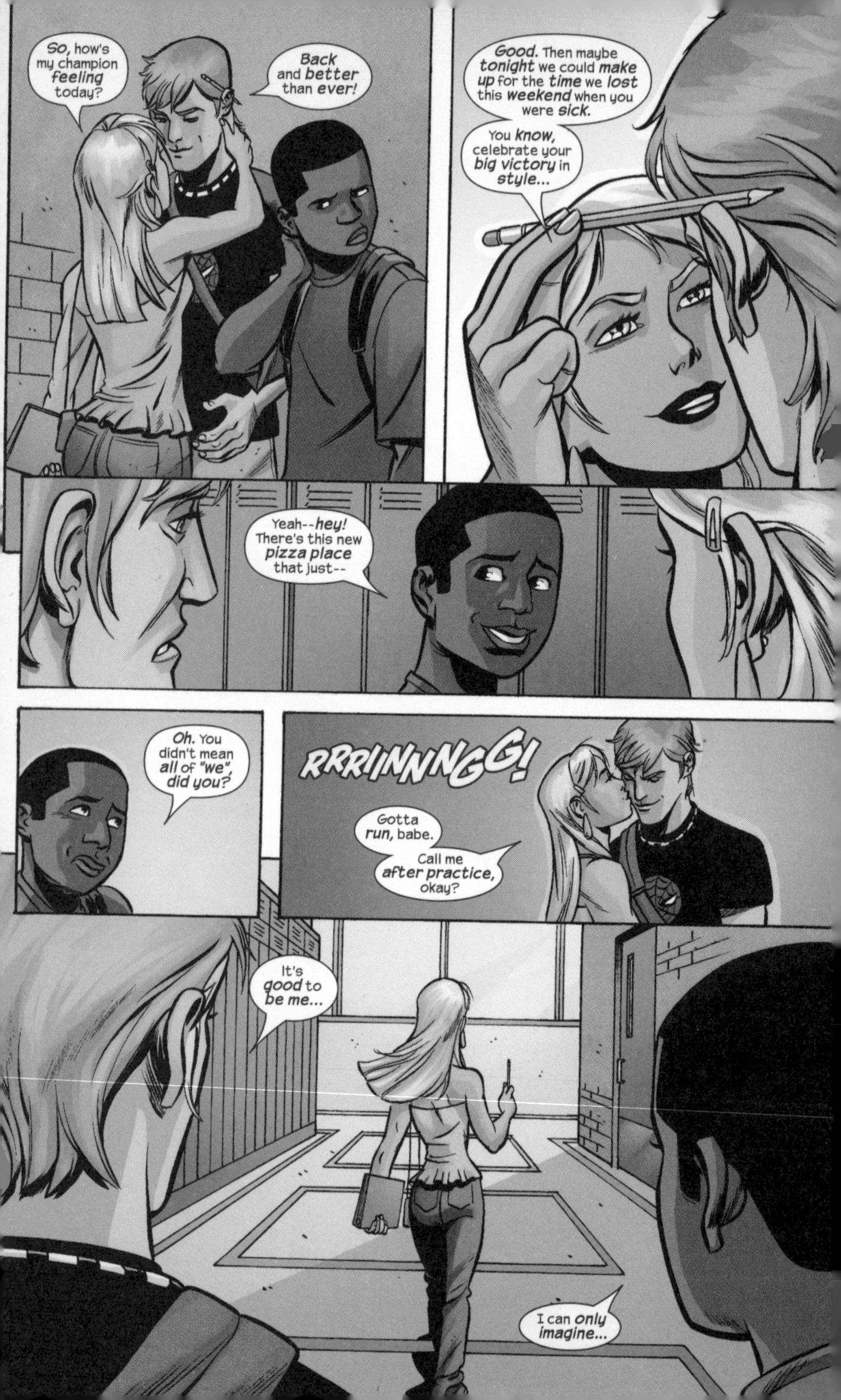
So, how's my champion feeling today?
Back and better than ever!
Good. Then maybe tonight we could make up for the time we lost this weekend when you were sick.
You know, celebrate your big victory in style...
Yeah--hey! There's this new pizza place that just--
Oh. You didn't mean all of "we", did you?
RRRIINNNGGG!
Gotta run, babe.
Call me after practice, okay?
It's good to be me...
I can only imagine...

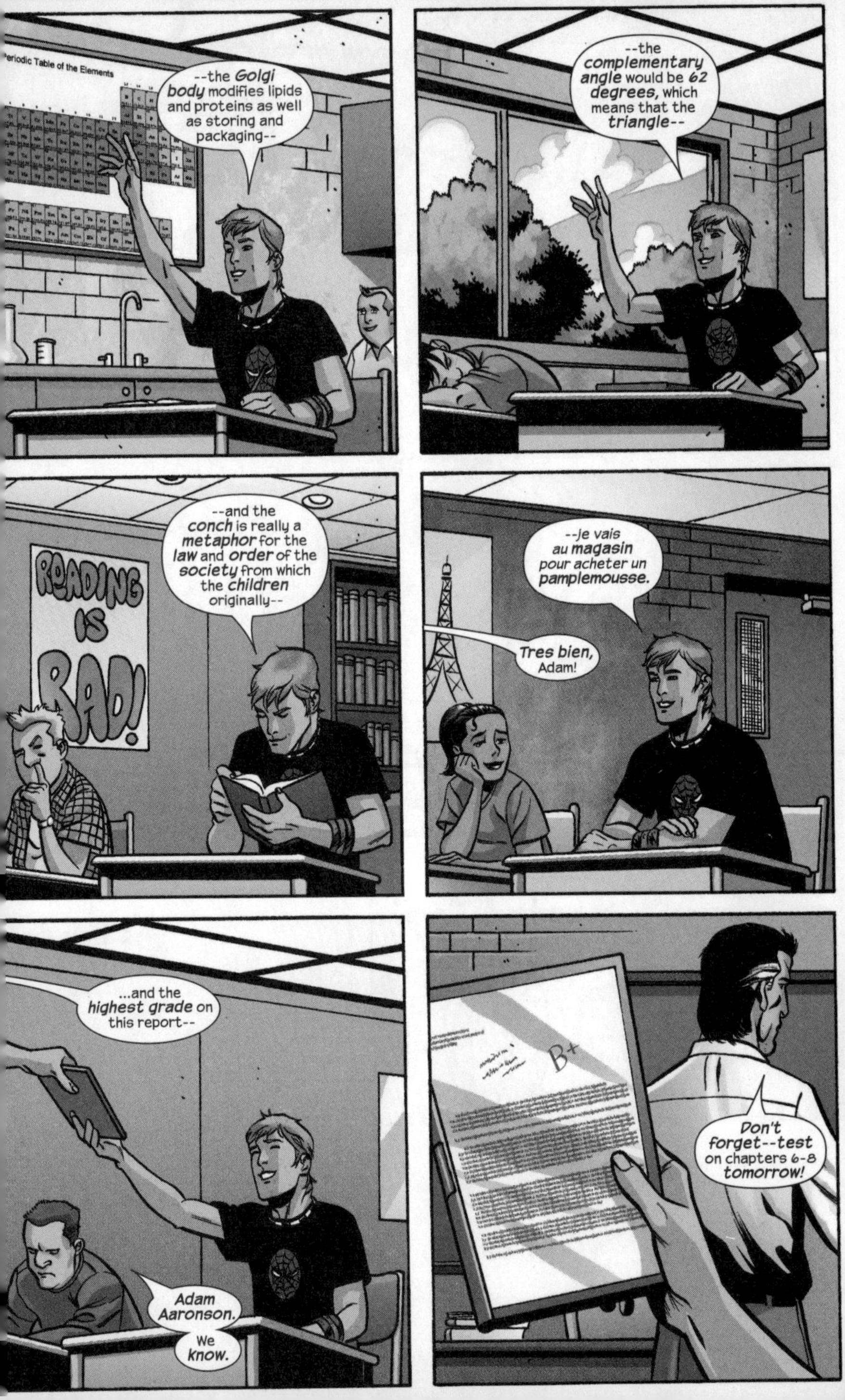
Periodic Table of the Elements
--the Golgi body modifies lipids and proteins as well as storing and packaging--
--the complementary angle would be 62 degrees, which means that the triangle--
READING IS RAD!
--and the conch is really a metaphor for the law and order of the society from which the children originally--
--je vais au magasin pour acheter un pamplemousse.
Tres bien, Adam!
...and the highest grade on this report--
Adam Aaronson.
We know.
B+
Don't forget--test on chapters 6-8 tomorrow!

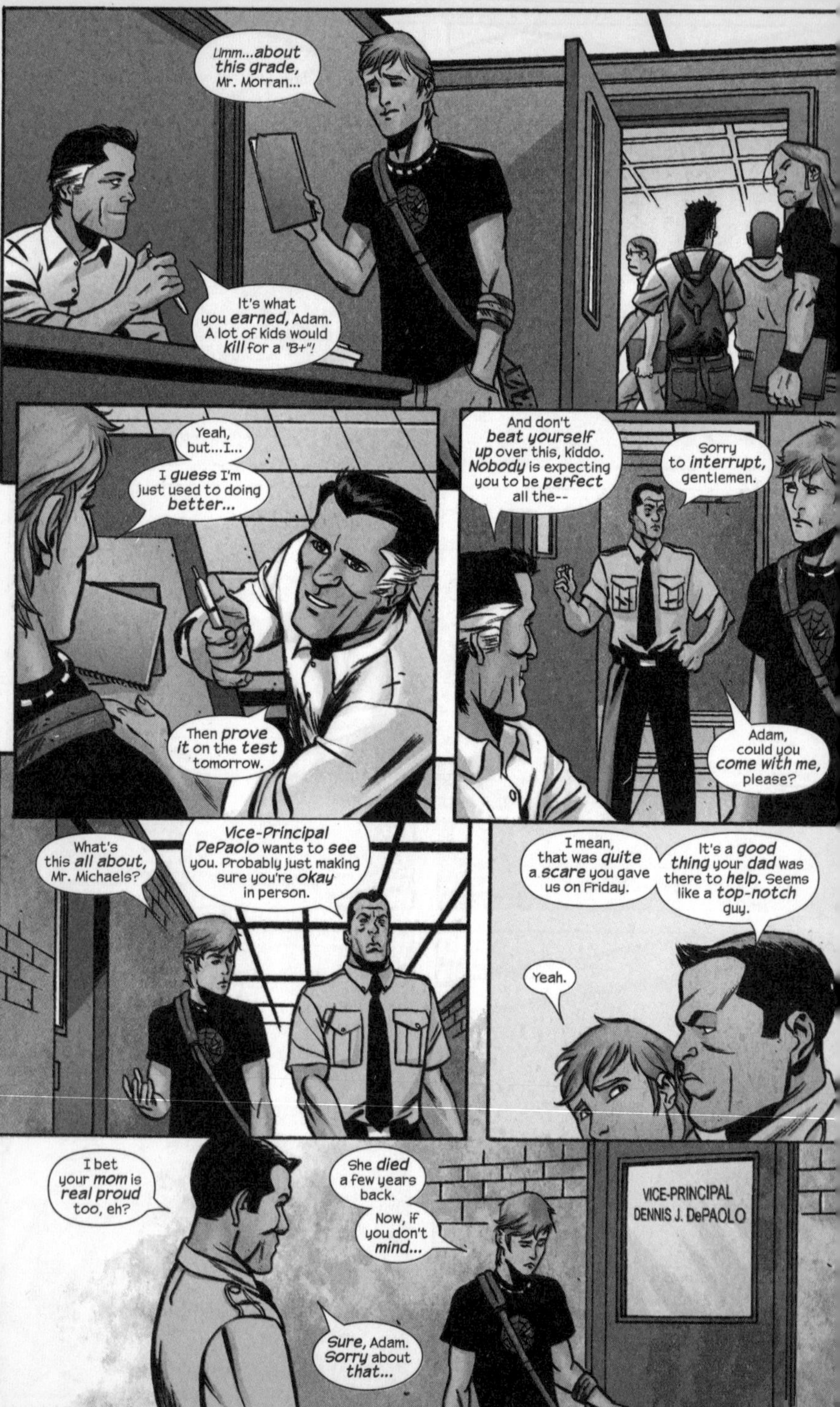
Umm...about this grade, Mr. Morran...
It's what you earned, Adam. A lot of kids would kill for a "B+"!
Yeah, but...I...
I guess I'm just used to doing better...
Then prove it on the test tomorrow.
And don't beat yourself up over this, kiddo. Nobody is expecting you to be perfect all the--
Sorry to interrupt, gentlemen.
Adam, could you come with me, please?
What's this all about, Mr. Michaels?
Vice-Principal DePaolo wants to see you. Probably just making sure you're okay in person.
I mean, that was quite a scare you gave us on Friday.
It's a good thing your dad was there to help. Seems like a top-notch guy.
Yeah.
I bet your mom is real proud too, eh?
She died a few years back.
Now, if you don't mind...
VICE-PRINCIPAL
DENNIS J. DePAOLO
Sure, Adam. Sorry about that...

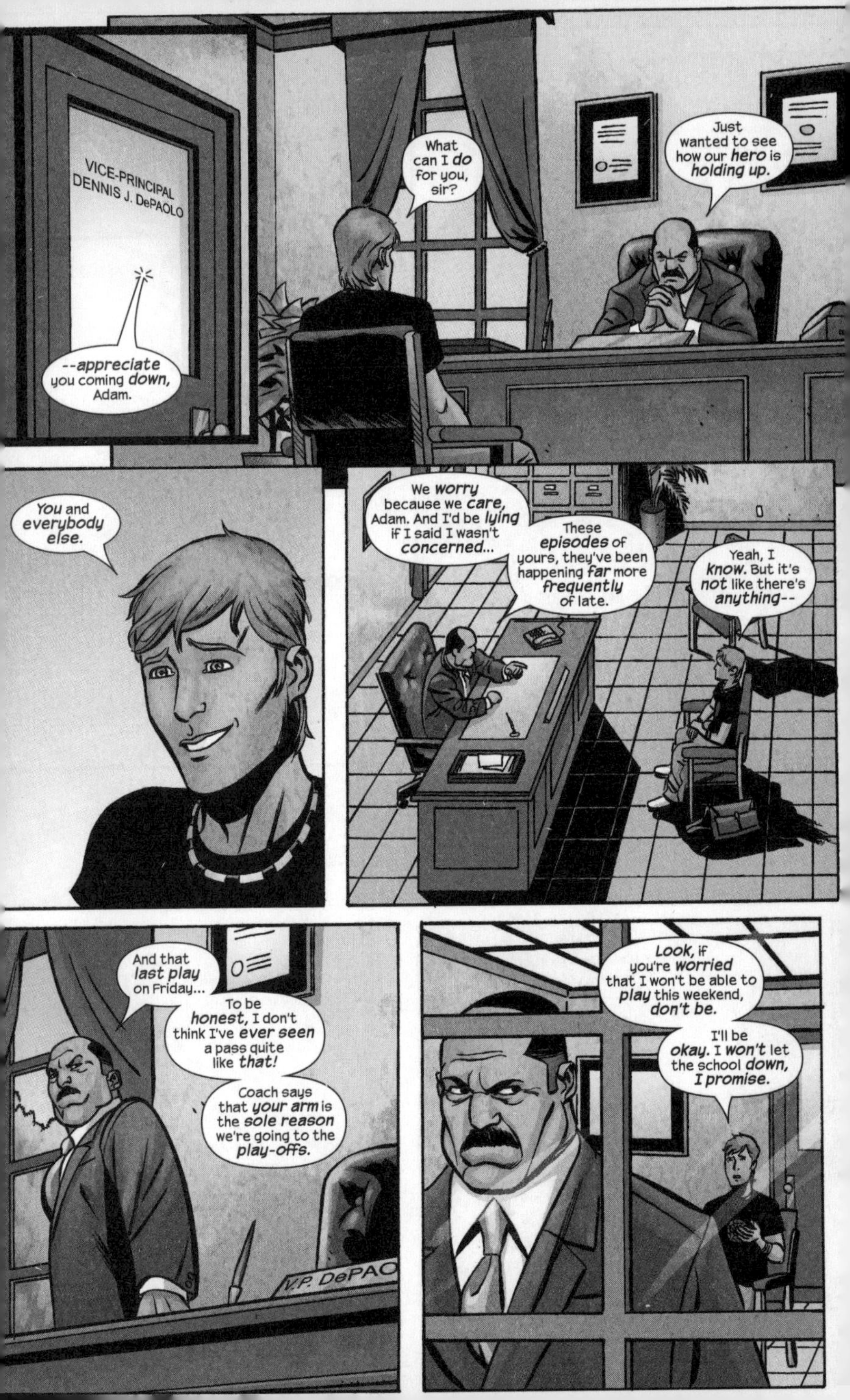
VICE-PRINCIPAL
DENNIS J. DePAOLO
--appreciate you coming down, Adam.
What can I do for you, sir?
Just wanted to see how our hero is holding up.
You and everybody else.
We worry because we care, Adam. And I'd be lying if I said I wasn't concerned...
These episodes of yours, they've been happening far more frequently of late.
Yeah, I know. But it's not like there's anything--
And that last play on Friday...
To be honest, I don't think I've ever seen a pass quite like that!
Coach says that your arm is the sole reason we're going to the play-offs.
V.P. DePAO
Look, if you're worried that I won't be able to play this weekend, don't be.
I'll be okay. I won't let the school down, I promise.

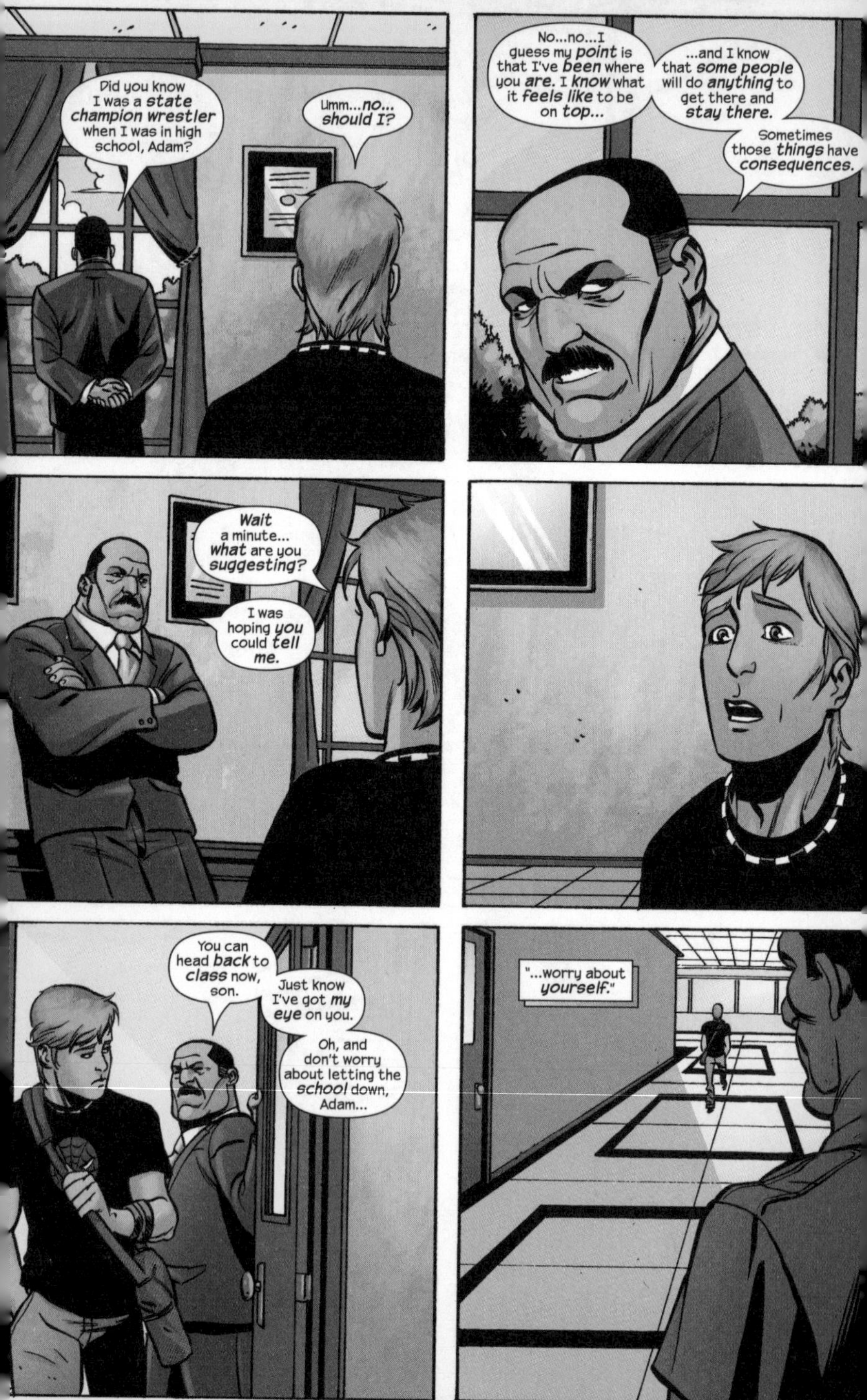

Did you know I was a state champion wrestler when I was in high school, Adam?
Umm...no... should I?
No...no...I guess my point is that I've been where you are. I know what it feels like to be on top...
...and I know that some people will do anything to get there and stay there.
Sometimes those things have consequences.
Wait a minute... what are you suggesting?
I was hoping you could tell me.
You can head back to class now, son.
Just know I've got my eye on you.
Oh, and don't worry about letting the school down, Adam...
"...worry about yourself."

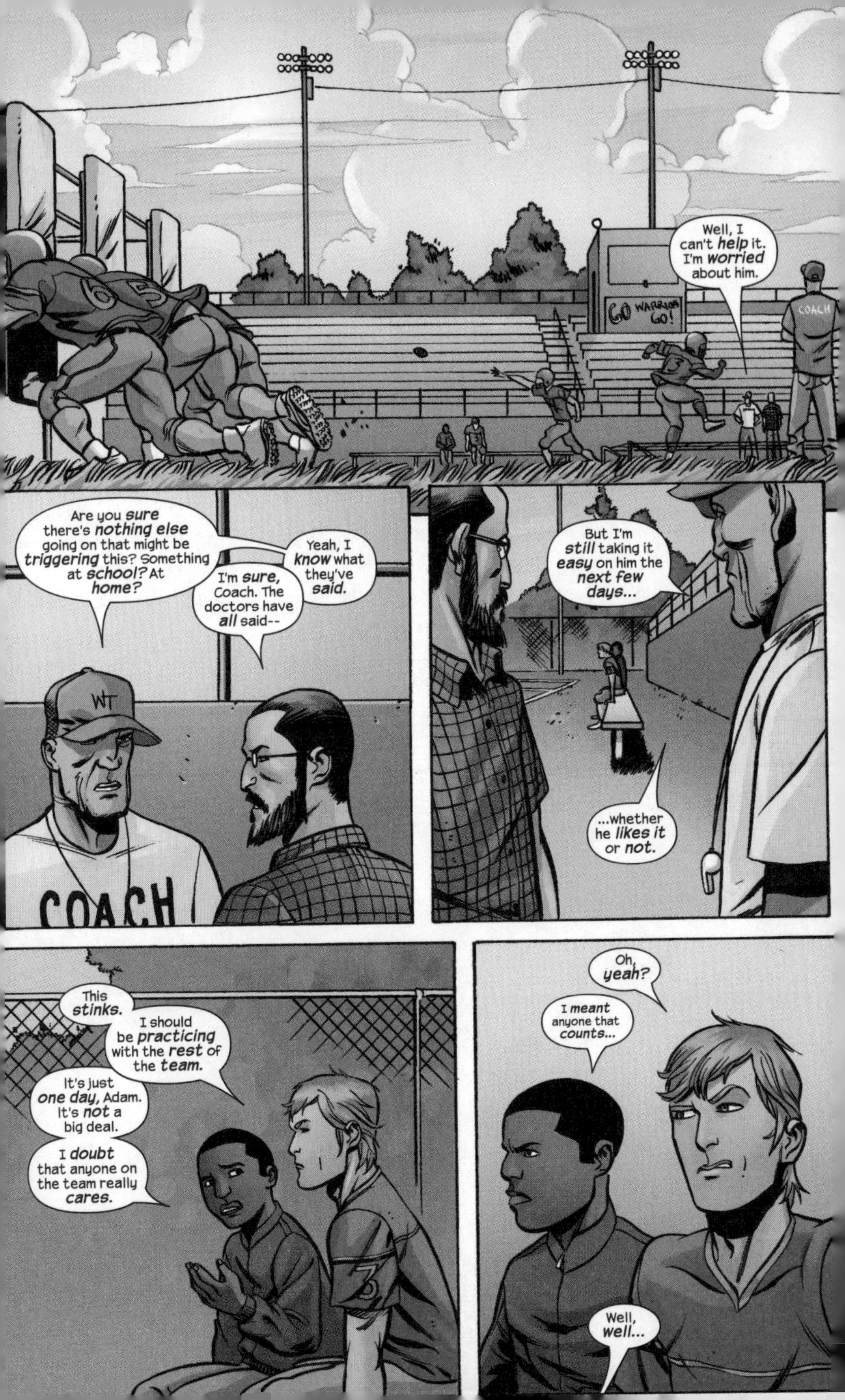
GO WARRIORS GO!
COACH
Well, I can't help it. I'm worried about him.
Are you sure there's nothing else going on that might be triggering this? Something at school? At home?
I'm sure, Coach. The doctors have all said--
Yeah, I know what they've said.
WT
COACH
But I'm still taking it easy on him the next few days...
...whether he likes it or not.
This stinks.
I should be practicing with the rest of the team.
It's just one day, Adam. It's not a big deal.
I doubt that anyone on the team really cares.
Oh, yeah?
I meant anyone that counts...
Well, well...

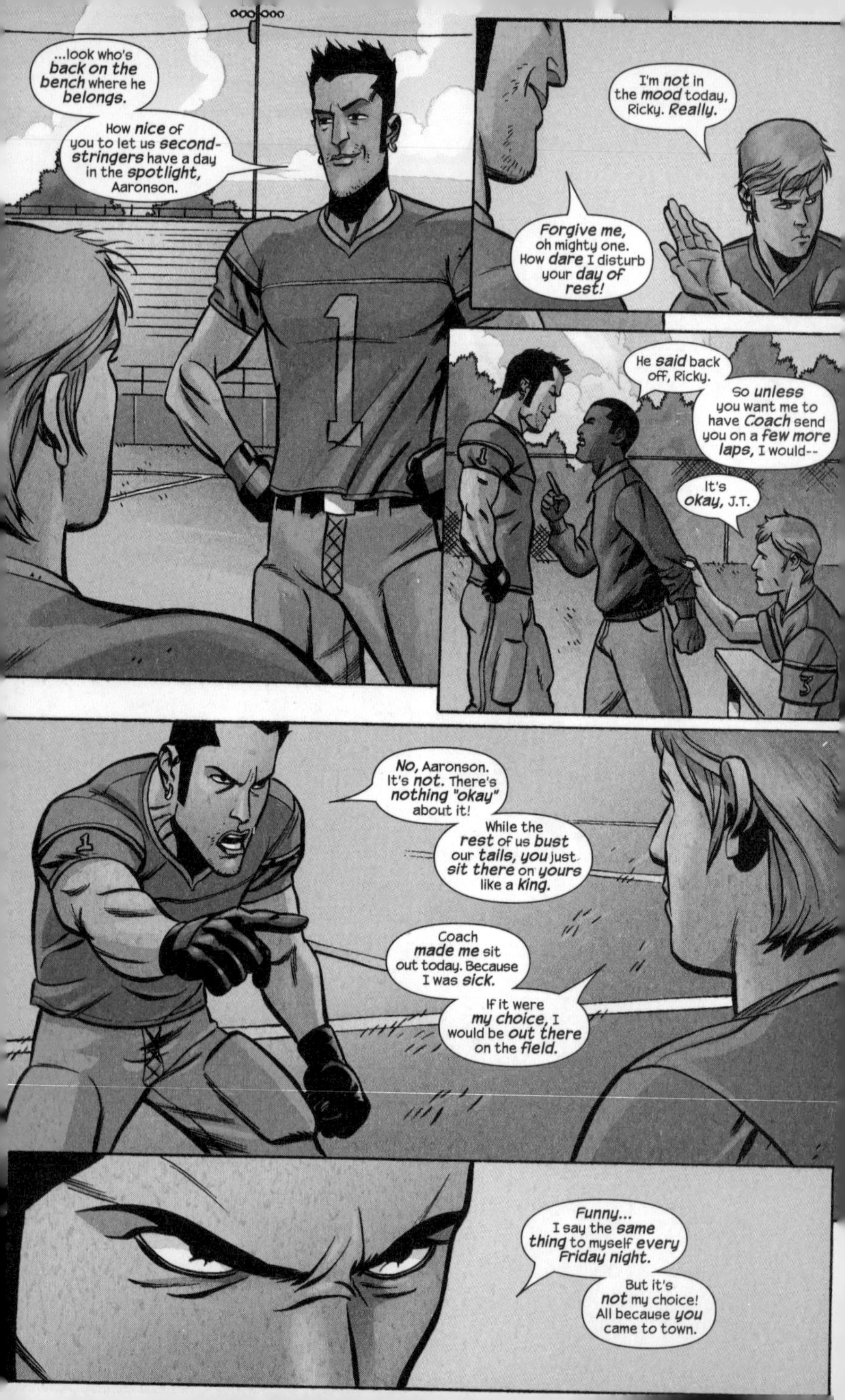
...look who's back on the bench where he belongs.
How nice of you to let us second-stringers have a day in the spotlight, Aaronson.
I'm not in the mood today, Ricky. Really.
Forgive me, oh mighty one. How dare I disturb your day of rest!
He said back off, Ricky.
So unless you want me to have Coach send you on a few more laps, I would--
It's okay, J.T.
No, Aaronson. It's not. There's nothing "okay" about it!
While the rest of us bust our tails, you just sit there on yours like a king.
Coach made me sit out today. Because I was sick.
If it were my choice, I would be out there on the field.
Funny... I say the same thing to myself every Friday night.
But it's not my choice! All because you came to town.

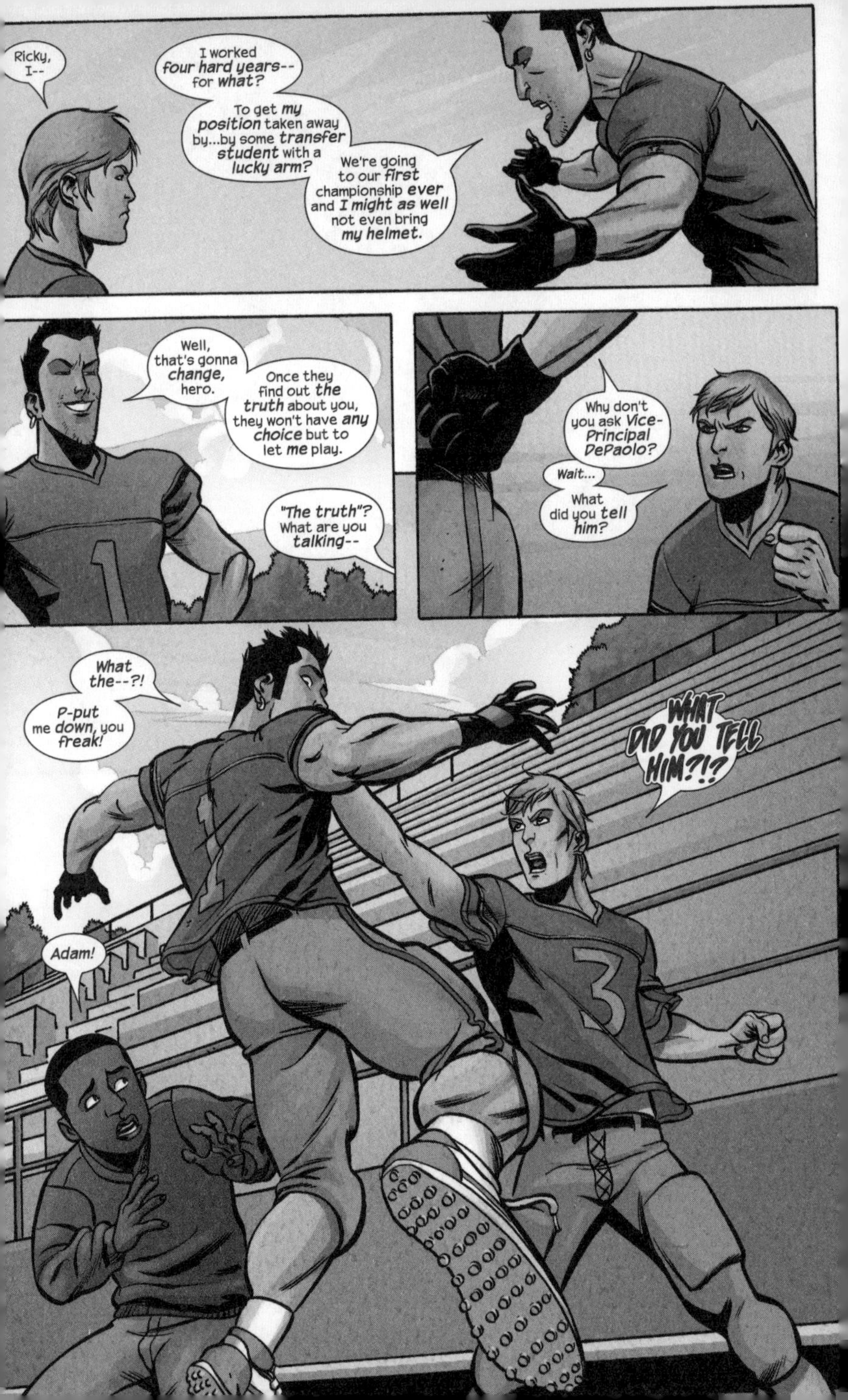
Ricky, I--
I worked four hard years-- for what?
To get my position taken away by...by some transfer student with a lucky arm?
We're going to our first championship ever and I might as well not even bring my helmet.
Well, that's gonna change, hero.
Once they find out the truth about you, they won't have any choice but to let me play.
"The truth"? What are you talking--
Why don't you ask Vice-Principal DePaolo?
Wait...
What did you tell him?
What the--?!
P-put me down, you freak!
WHAT DID YOU TELL HIM?!?
Adam!

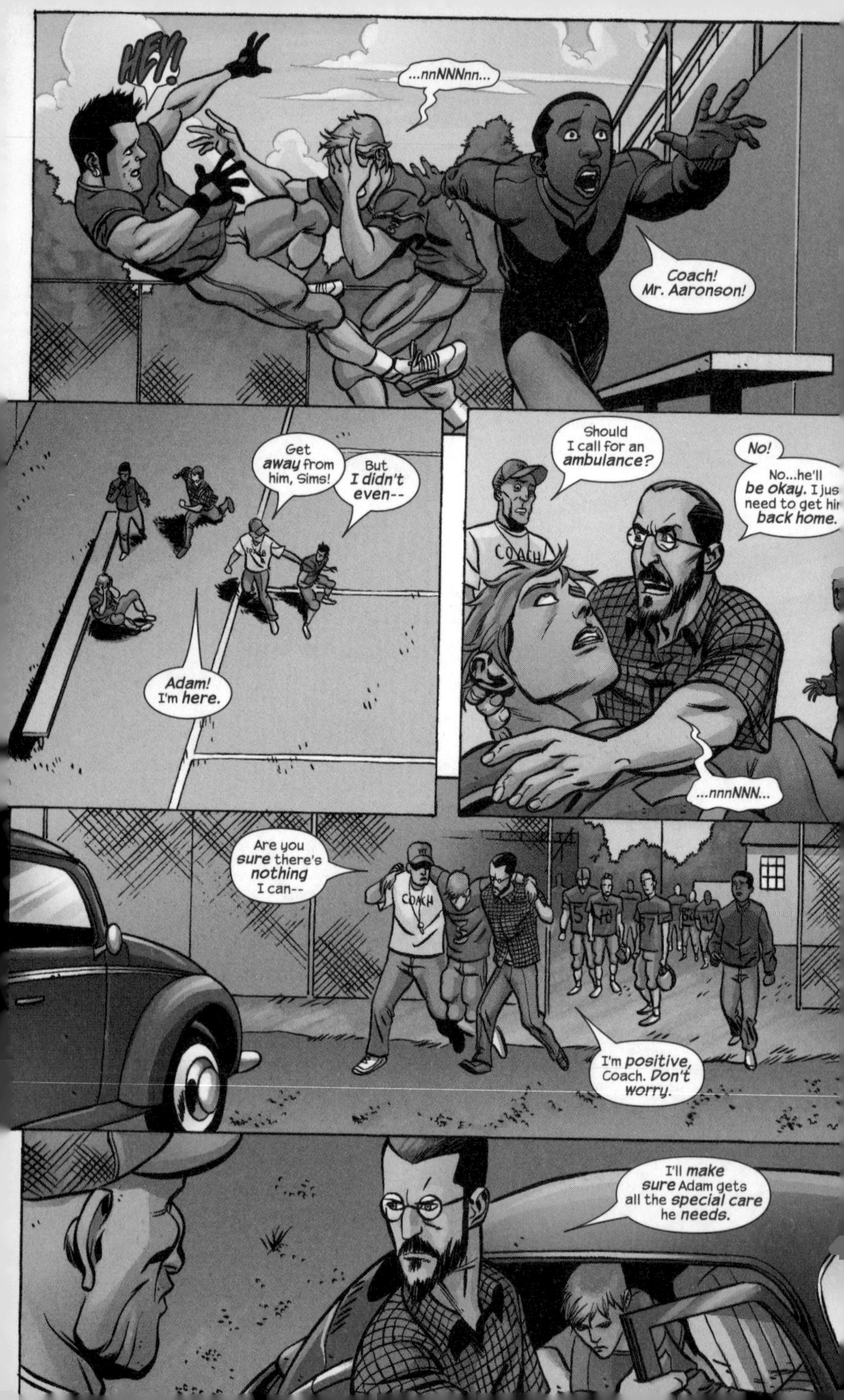
HEY!
...nnNNNnn...
Coach! Mr. Aaronson!
Get away from him, Sims!
But I didn't even--
Adam! I'm here.
Should I call for an ambulance?
No!
No...he'll be okay. I jus need to get hir back home.
...nnnNNN...
Are you sure there's nothing I can--
I'm positive, Coach. Don't worry.
I'll make sure Adam gets all the special care he needs.

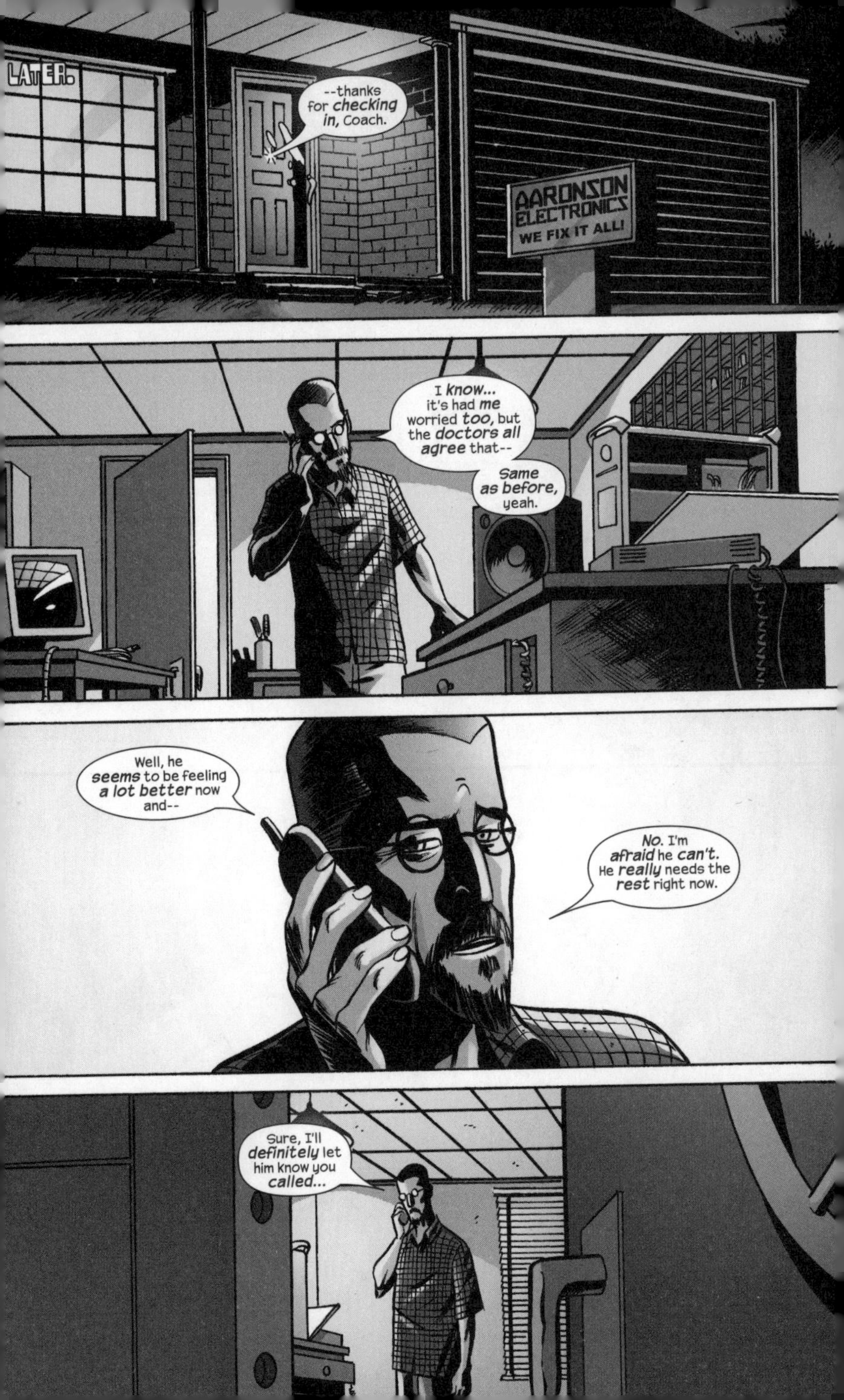
LATER.
--thanks for checking in, Coach.
AARONSON ELECTRONICS WE FIX IT ALL!
I know... it's had me worried too, but the doctors all agree that--
Same as before, yeah.
Well, he seems to be feeling a lot better now and--
No. I'm afraid he can't. He really needs the rest right now.
Sure, I'll definitely let him know you called...

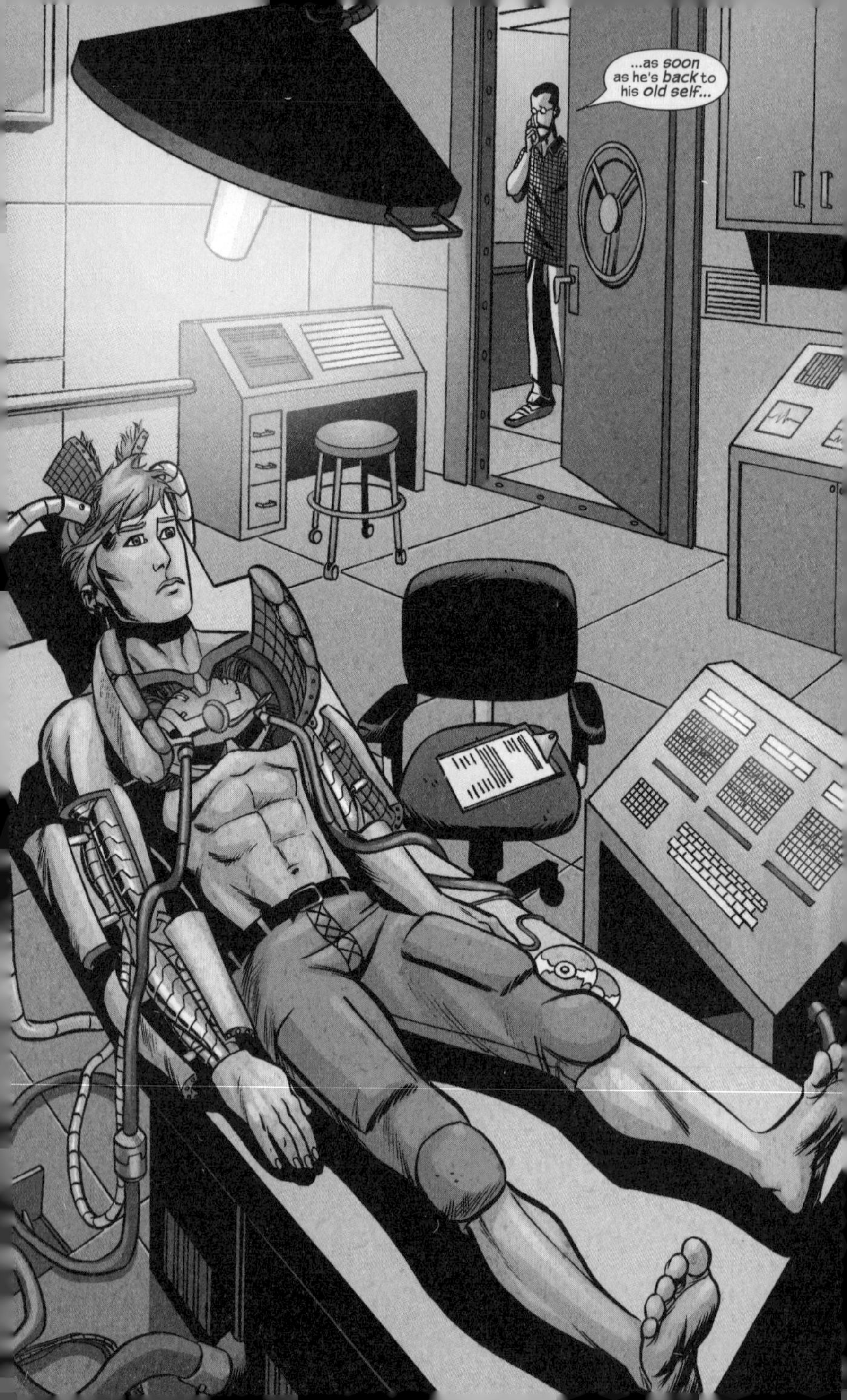
...as soon as he's back to his old self...

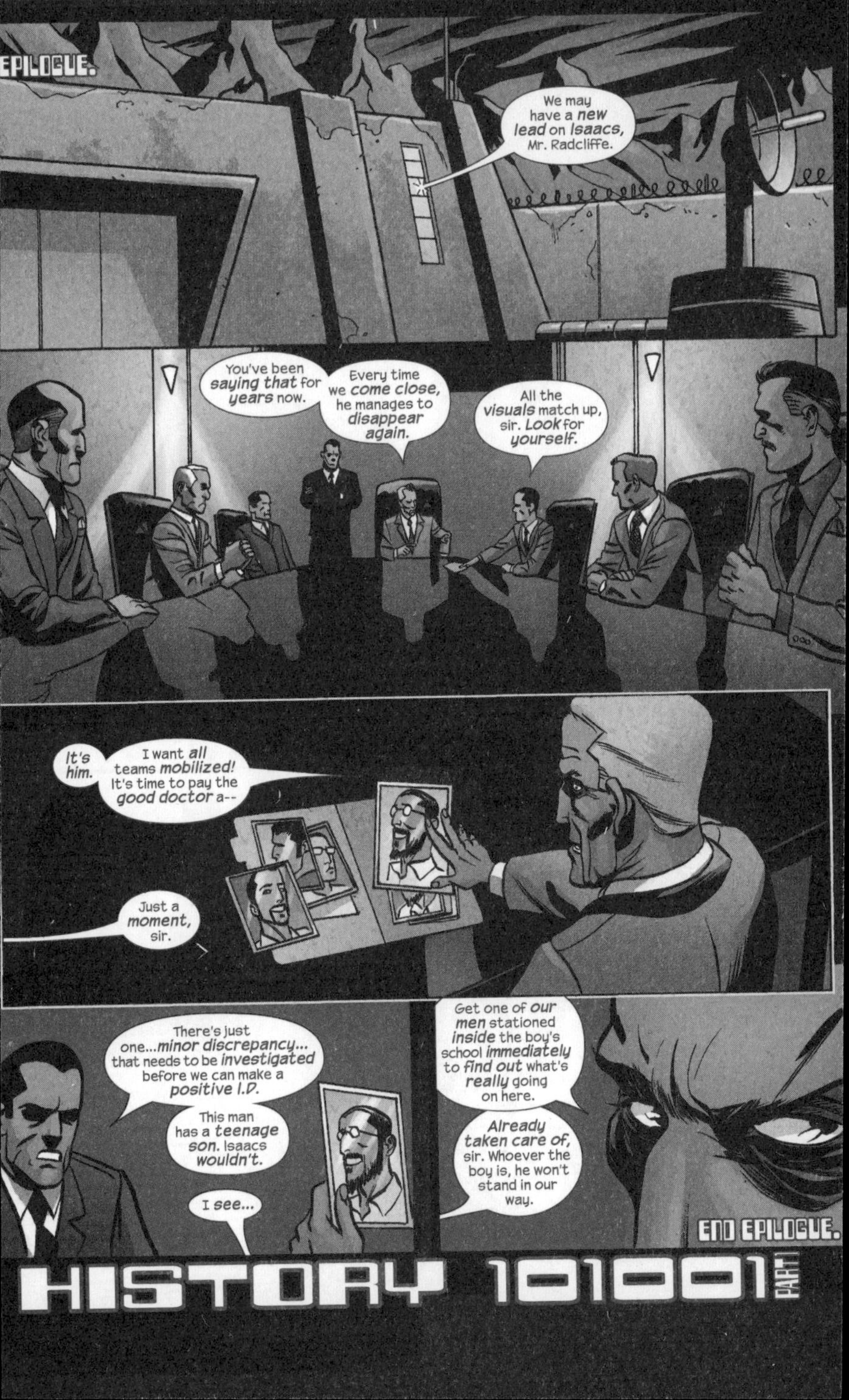
EPILOGUE.
We may have a new lead on Isaacs, Mr. Radcliffe.
You've been saying that for years now.
Every time we come close, he manages to disappear again.
All the visuals match up, sir. Look for yourself.
It's him.
I want all teams mobilized! It's time to pay the good doctor a--
Just a moment, sir.
There's just one...minor discrepancy... that needs to be investigated before we can make a positive I.D.
This man has a teenage son. Isaacs wouldn't.
I see...
Get one of our men stationed inside the boy's school immediately to find out what's really going on here.
Already taken care of, sir. Whoever the boy is, he won't stand in our way.
END EPILOGUE.
HISTORY 101001 PART 1

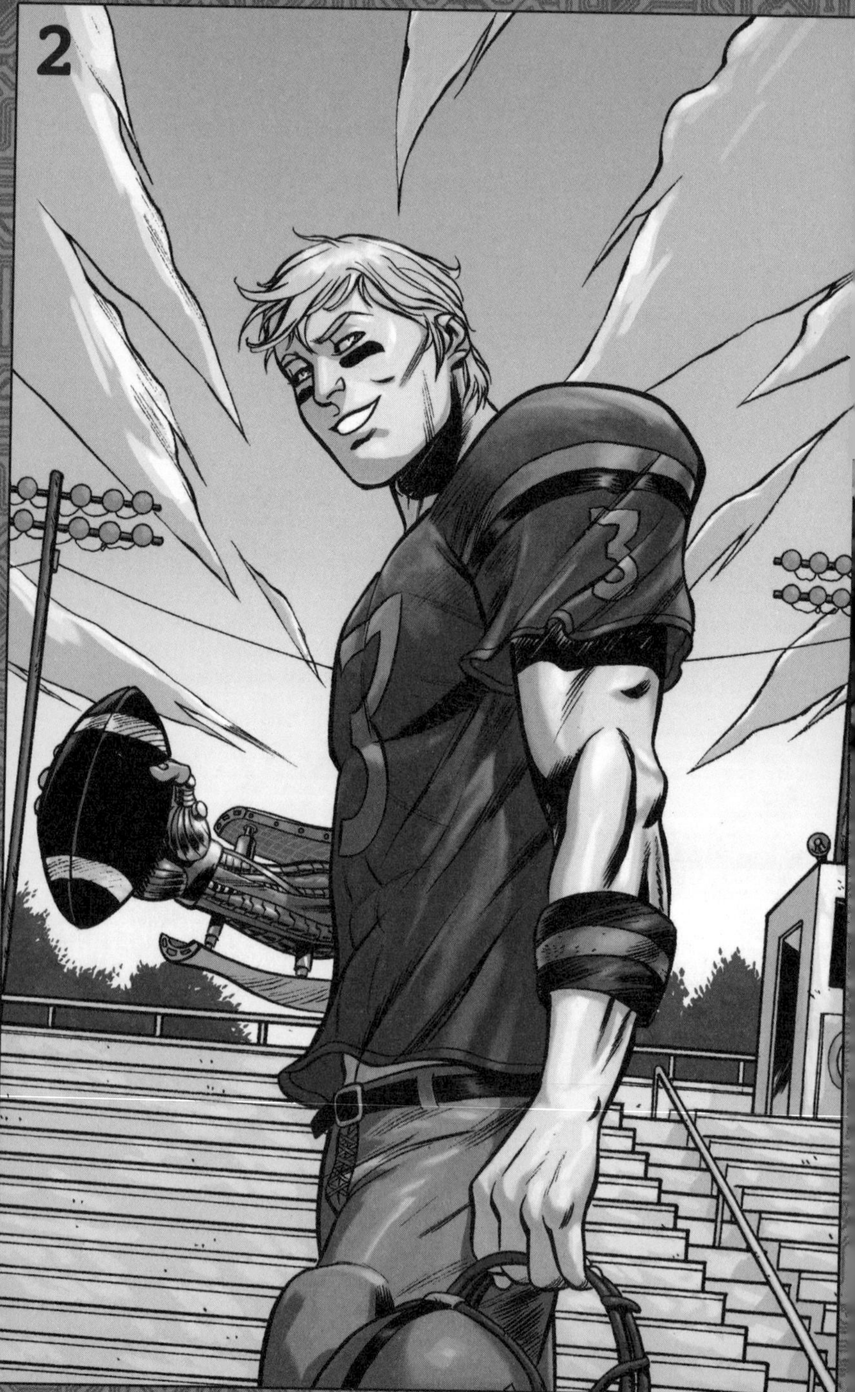

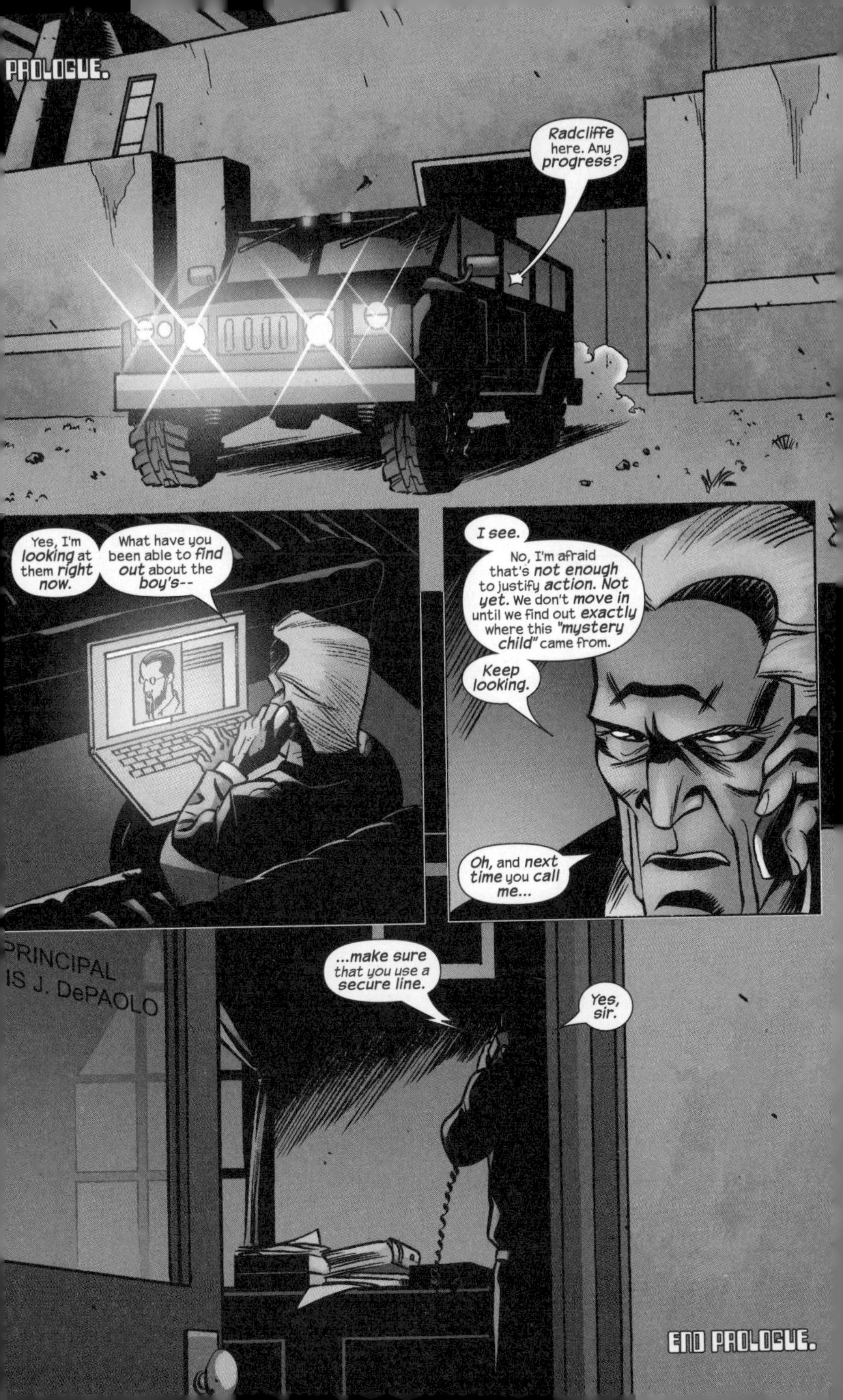
PROLOGUE.
Radcliffe here. Any progress?
Yes, I'm looking at them right now.
What have you been able to find out about the boy's--
I see.
No, I'm afraid that's not enough to justify action. Not yet. We don't move in until we find out exactly where this "mystery child" came from.
Keep looking.
Oh, and next time you call me...
PRINCIPAL
IS J. DePAOLO
...make sure that you use a secure line.
Yes, sir.
END PROLOGUE.

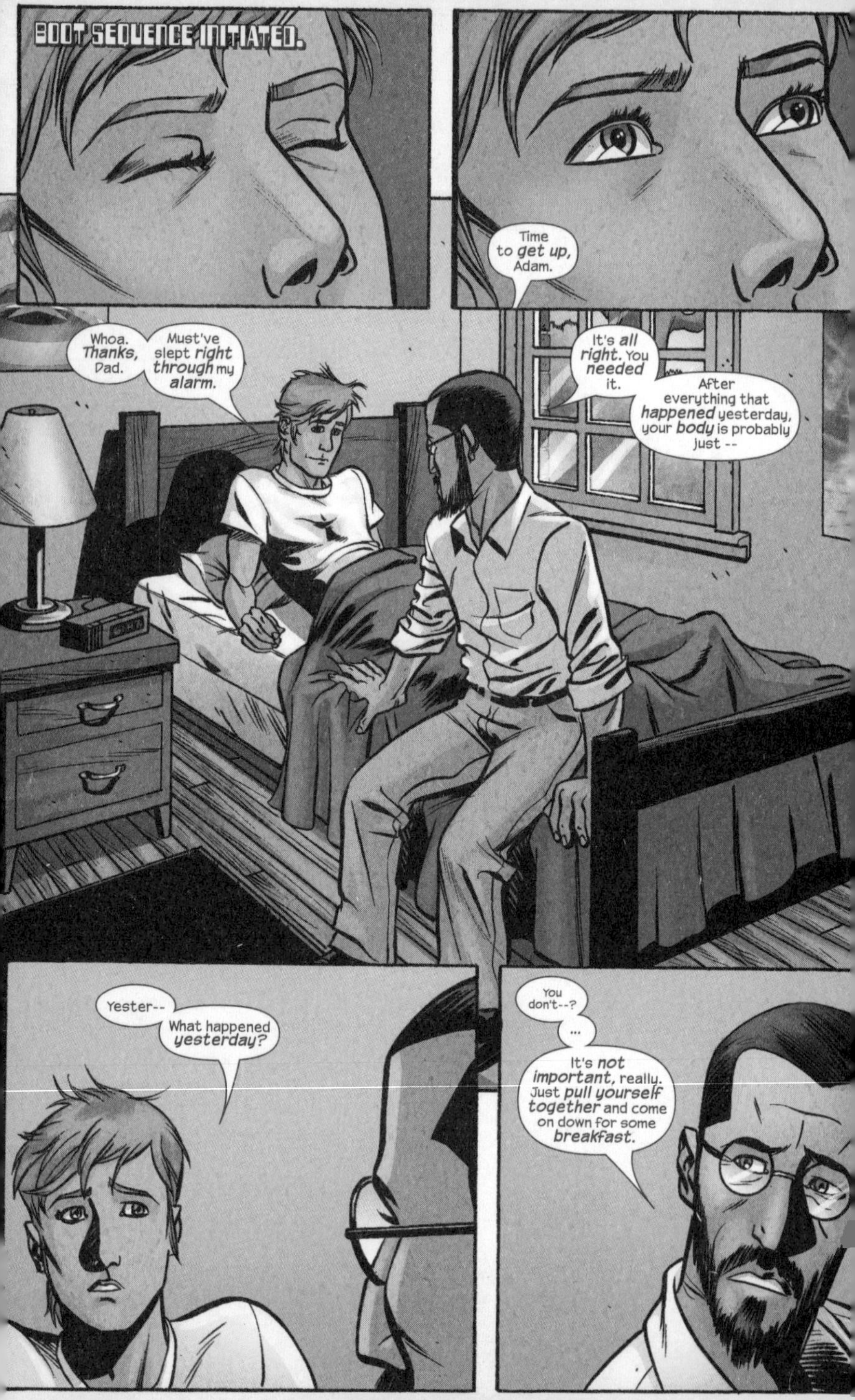
BOOT SEQUENCE INITIATED.
Time to get up, Adam.
Whoa. Thanks, Dad.
Must've slept right through my alarm.
It's all right. You needed it.
After everything that happened yesterday, your body is probably just --
Yester--
What happened yesterday?
You don't--?
...
It's not important, really. Just pull yourself together and come on down for some breakfast.

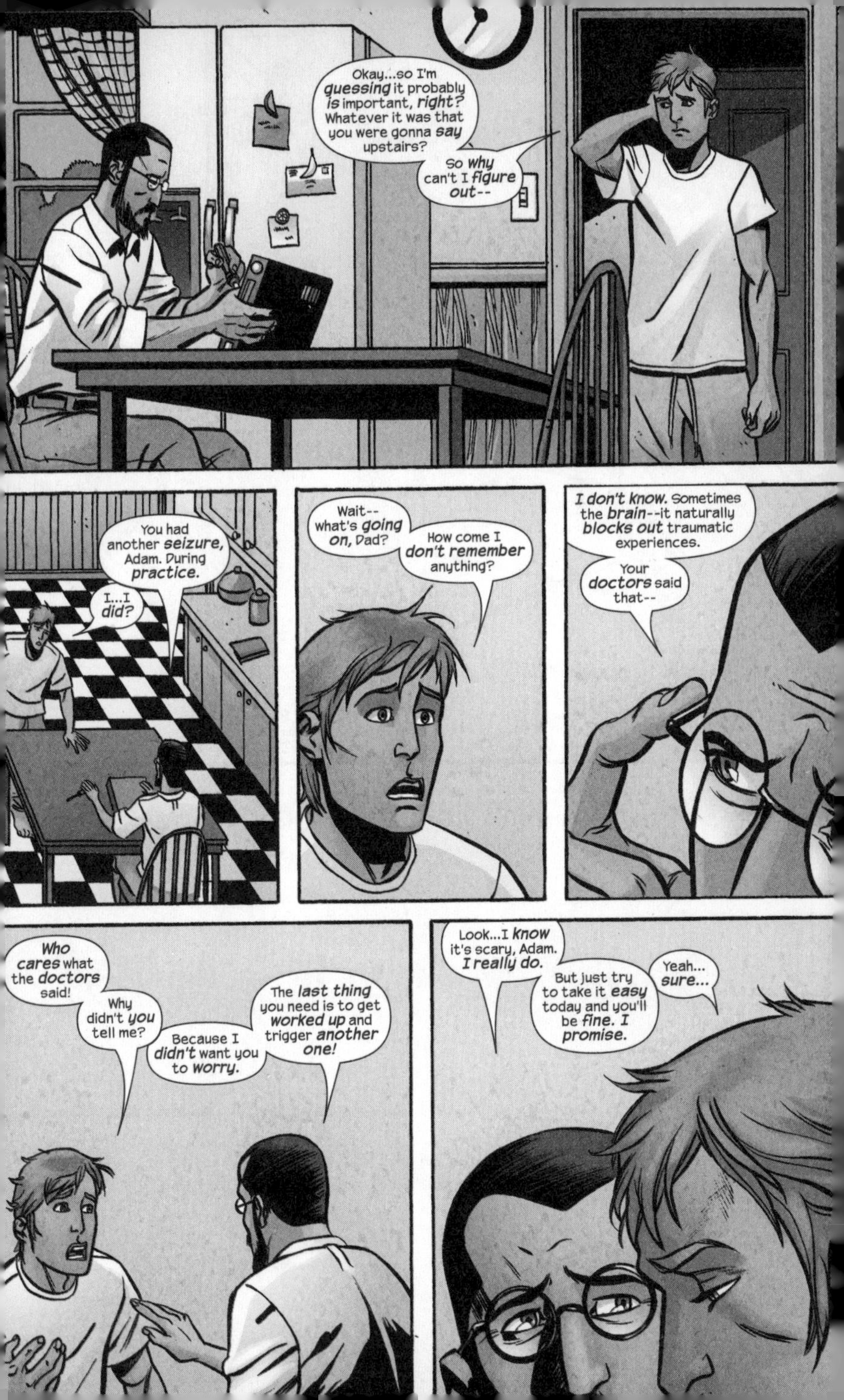
Okay...so I'm guessing it probably is important, right? Whatever it was that you were gonna say upstairs?
So why can't I figure out--
You had another seizure, Adam. During practice.
I...I did?
Wait--what's going on, Dad?
How come I don't remember anything?
I don't know. Sometimes the brain--it naturally blocks out traumatic experiences.
Your doctors said that--
Who cares what the doctors said!
Why didn't you tell me?
Because I didn't want you to worry.
The last thing you need is to get worked up and trigger another one!
Look...I know it's scary, Adam. I really do.
But just try to take it easy today and you'll be fine. I promise.
Yeah... sure...

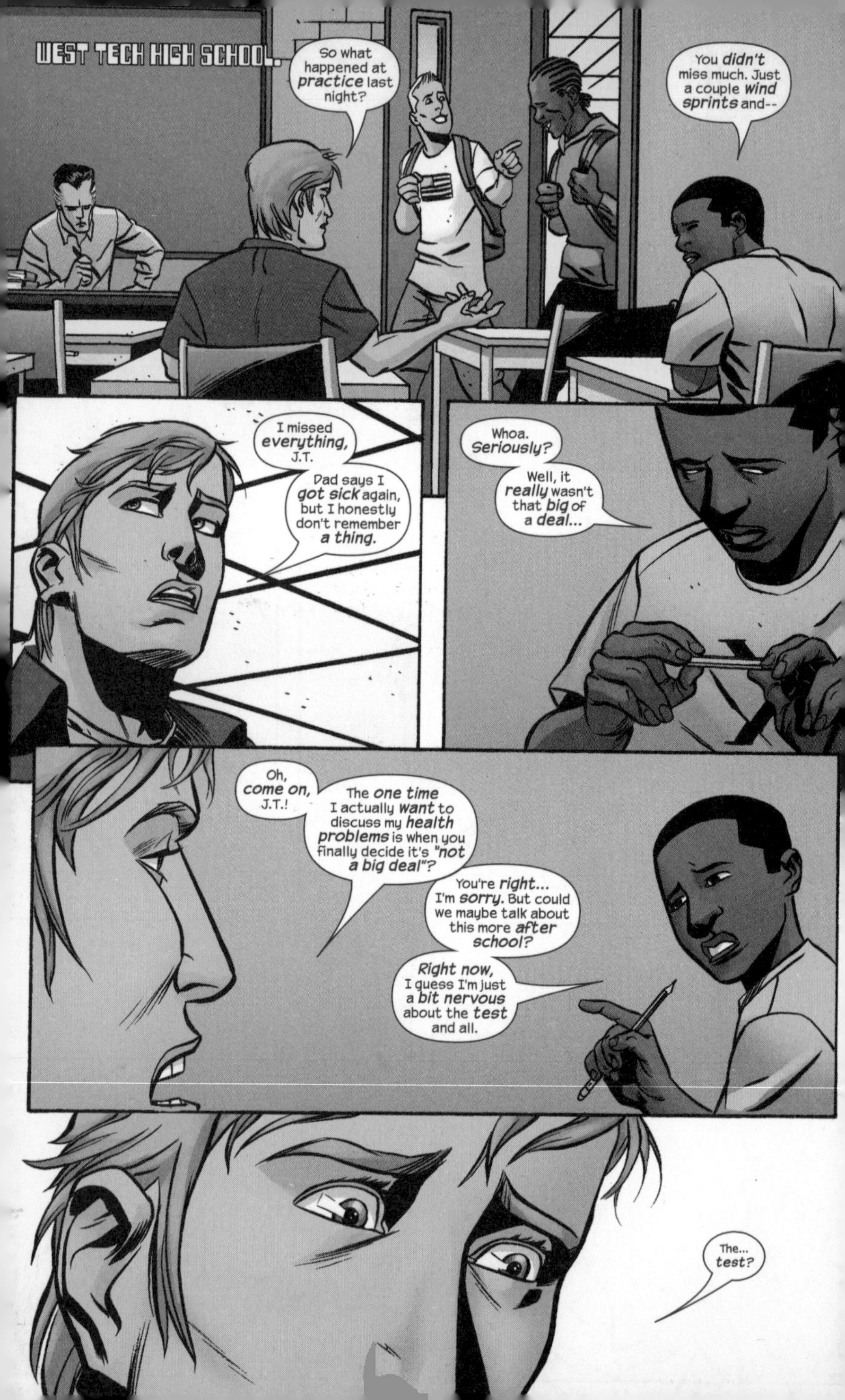
WEST TECH HIGH SCHOOL...
So what happened at practice last night?
You didn't miss much. Just a couple wind sprints and--
I missed everything, J.T.
Dad says I got sick again, but I honestly don't remember a thing.
Whoa. Seriously?
Well, it really wasn't that big of a deal...
Oh, come on, J.T.!
The one time I actually want to discuss my health problems is when you finally decide it's "not a big deal"?
You're right... I'm sorry. But could we maybe talk about this more after school?
Right now, I guess I'm just a bit nervous about the test and all.
The... test?

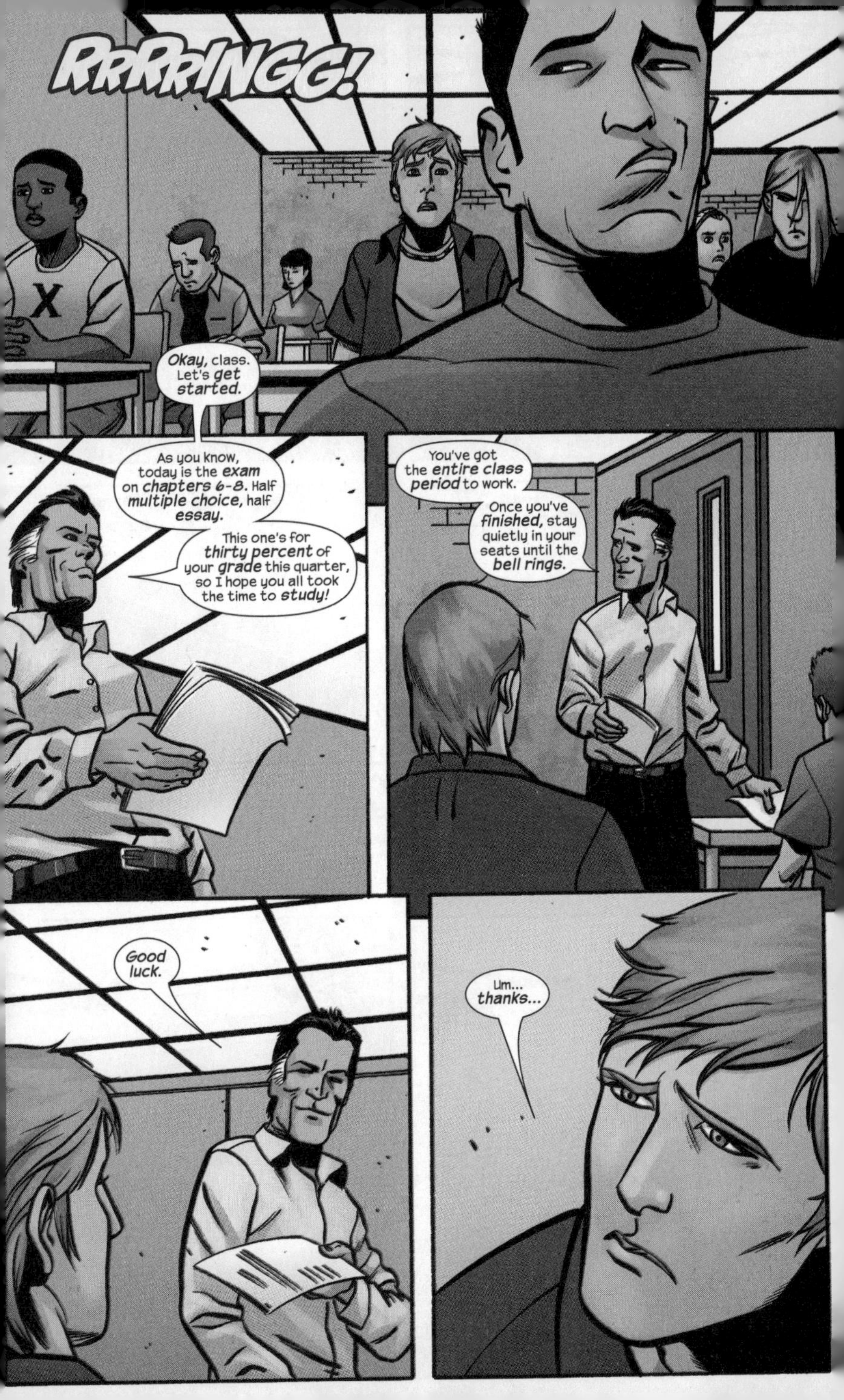
RRRRINGG!
Okay, class. Let's get started.
As you know, today is the exam on chapters 6-8. Half multiple choice, half essay.
This one's for thirty percent of your grade this quarter, so I hope you all took the time to study!
You've got the entire class period to work.
Once you've finished, stay quietly in your seats until the bell rings.
Good luck.
Um... thanks...

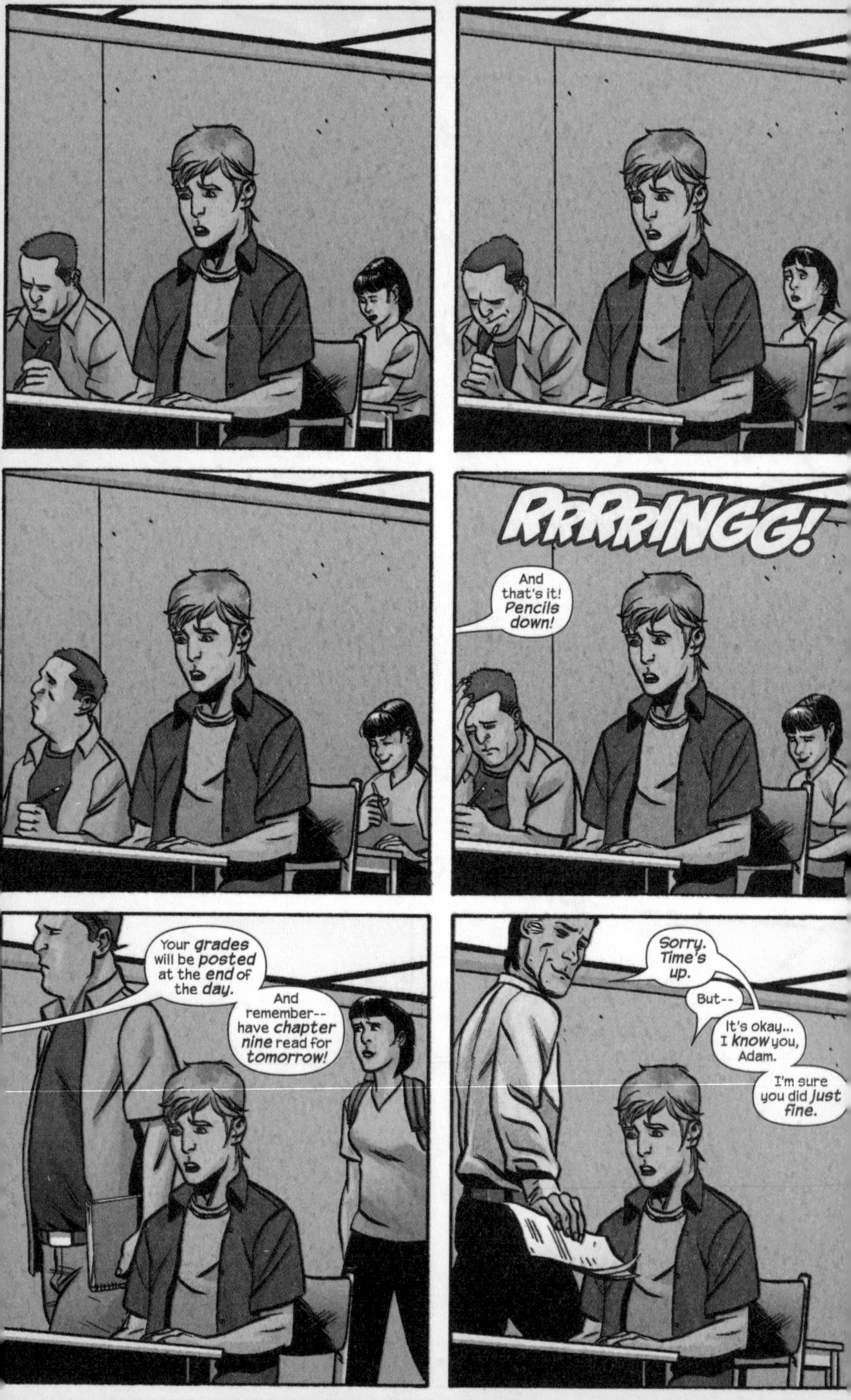
RRRRINGG!
And that's it! Pencils down!
Your grades will be posted at the end of the day.
And remember-- have chapter nine read for tomorrow!
Sorry. Time's up.
But--
It's okay... I know you, Adam.
I'm sure you did just fine.

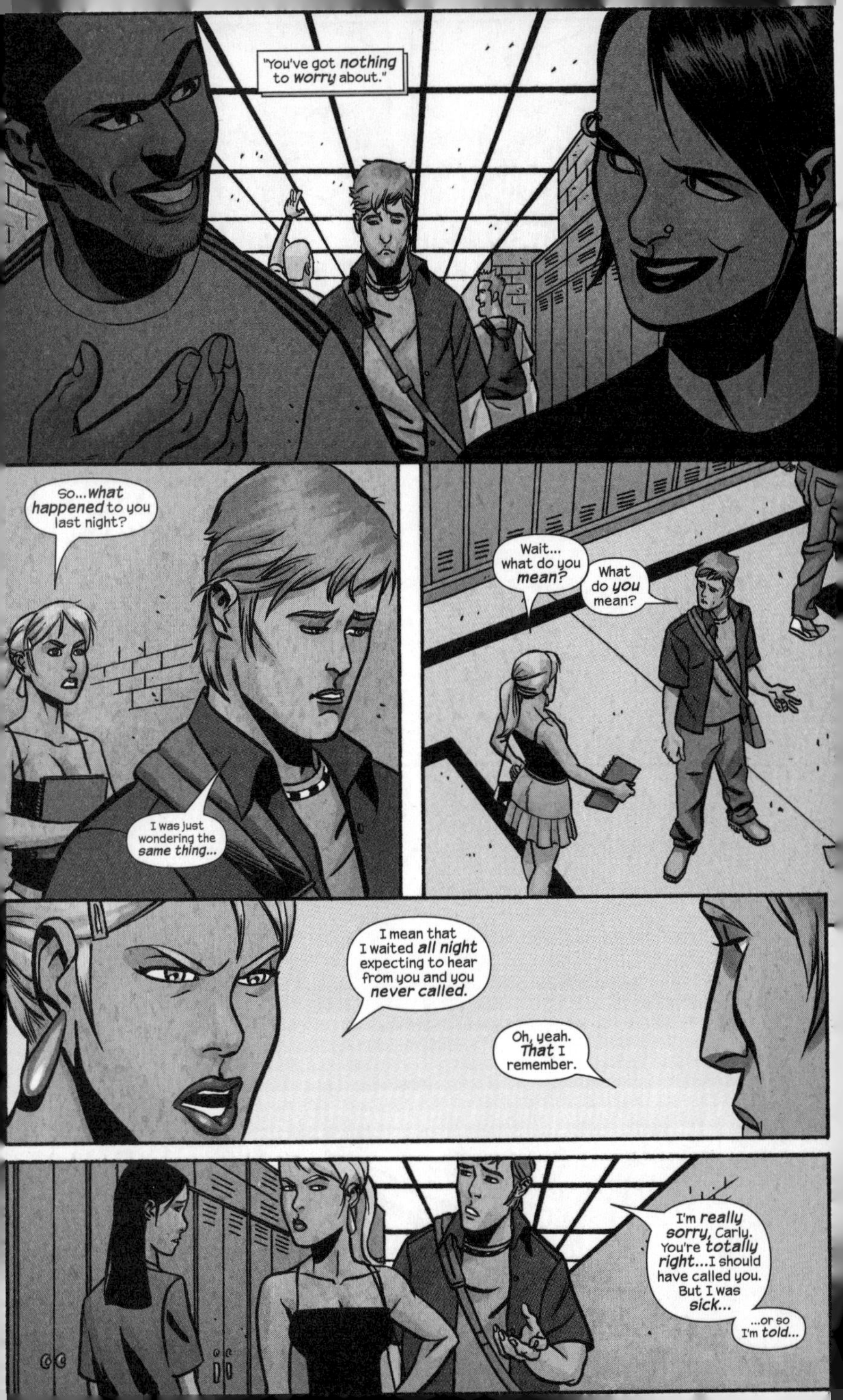

"You've got nothing to worry about."
So...what happened to you last night?
I was just wondering the same thing...
Wait... what do you mean?
What do you mean?
I mean that I waited all night expecting to hear from you and you never called.
Oh, yeah. That I remember.
I'm really sorry, Carly. You're totally right...I should have called you. But I was sick...
...or so I'm told...

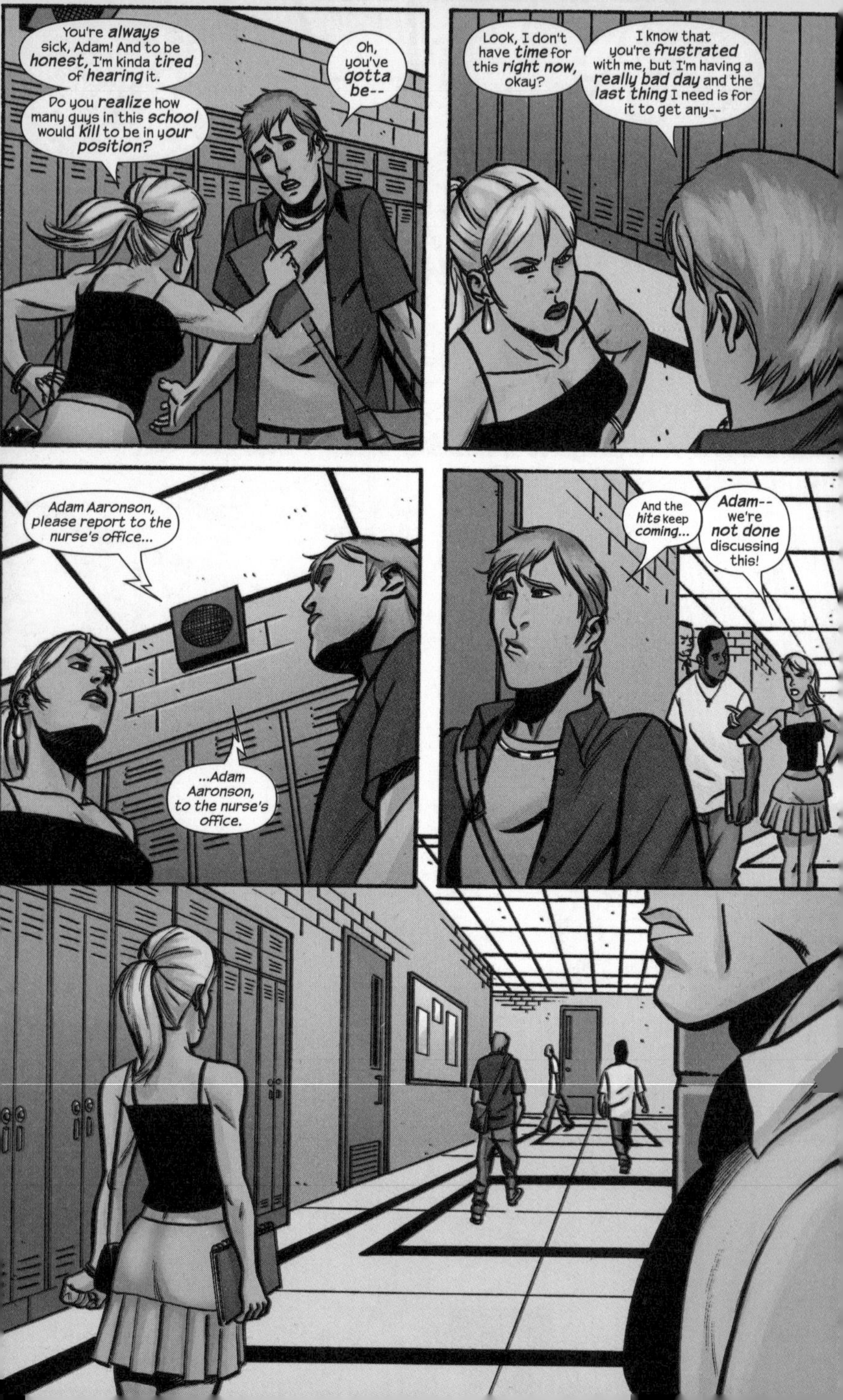
You're always sick, Adam! And to be honest, I'm kinda tired of hearing it.
Do you realize how many guys in this school would kill to be in your position?
Oh, you've gotta be--
Look, I don't have time for this right now, okay?
I know that you're frustrated with me, but I'm having a really bad day and the last thing I need is for it to get any--
Adam Aaronson, please report to the nurse's office...
...Adam Aaronson, to the nurse's office.
And the hits keep coming...
Adam-- we're not done discussing this!

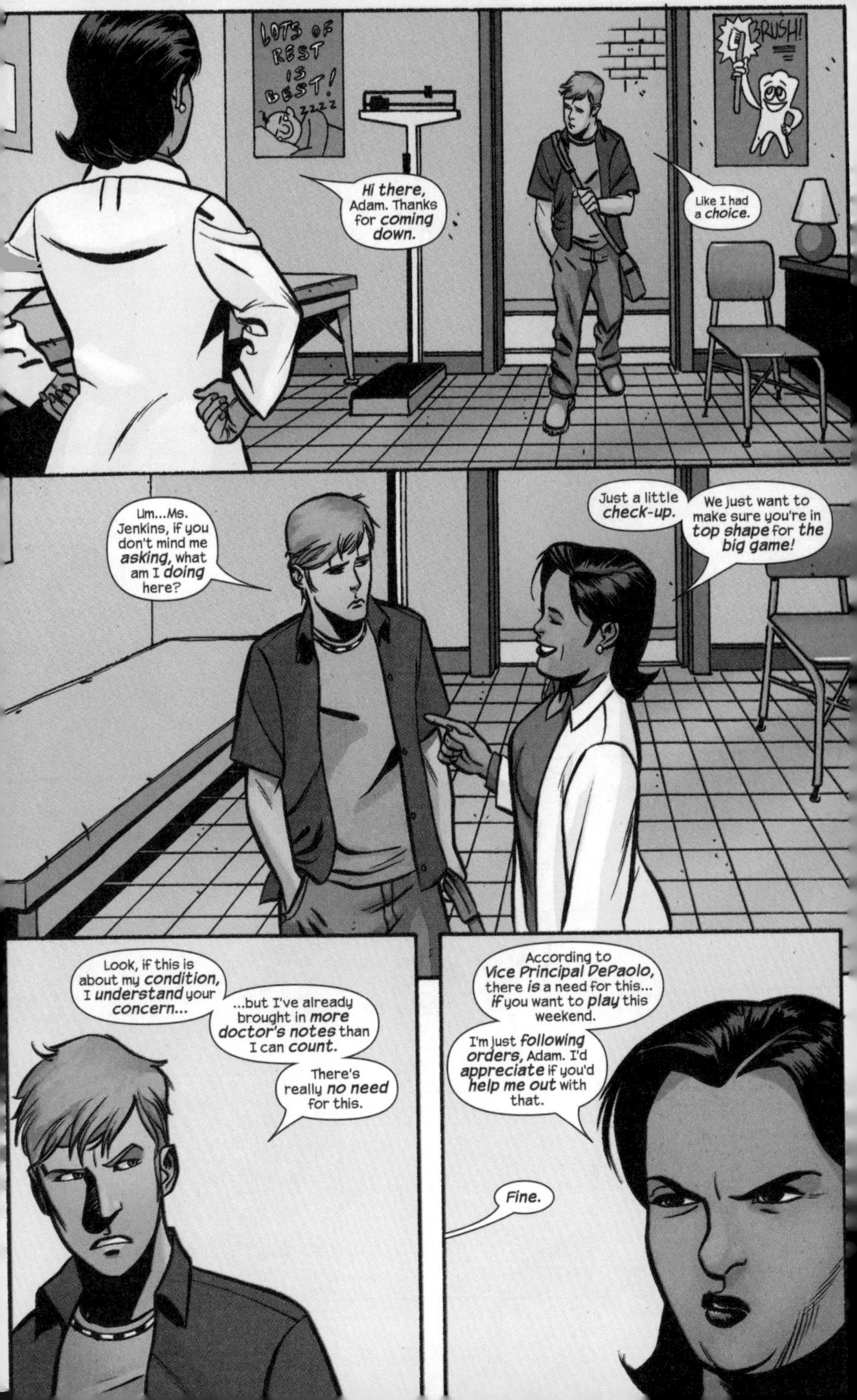
LOTS OF REST IS BEST!
ZZZZ
Hi there, Adam. Thanks for coming down.
BRUSH!
Like I had a choice.
Um...Ms. Jenkins, if you don't mind me asking, what am I doing here?
Just a little check-up.
We just want to make sure you're in top shape for the big game!
Look, if this is about my condition, I understand your concern...
...but I've already brought in more doctor's notes than I can count.
There's really no need for this.
According to Vice Principal DePaolo, there is a need for this... if you want to play this weekend.
I'm just following orders, Adam. I'd appreciate if you'd help me out with that.
Fine.

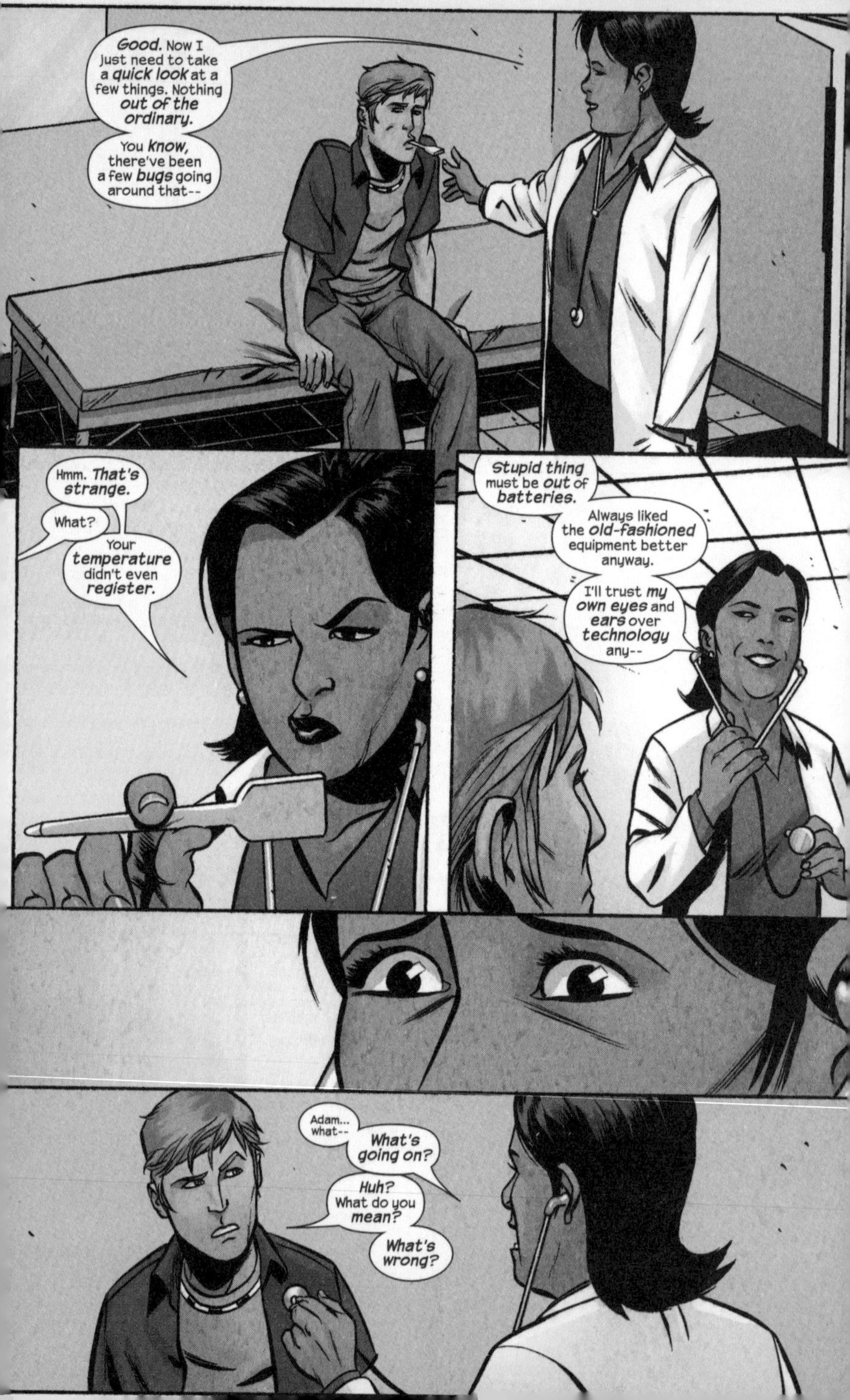
Good. Now I just need to take a quick look at a few things. Nothing out of the ordinary.
You know, there've been a few bugs going around that--
Hmm. That's strange.
What?
Your temperature didn't even register.
Stupid thing must be out of batteries.
Always liked the old-fashioned equipment better anyway.
I'll trust my own eyes and ears over technology any--
Adam... what--
What's going on?
Huh? What do you mean?
What's wrong?

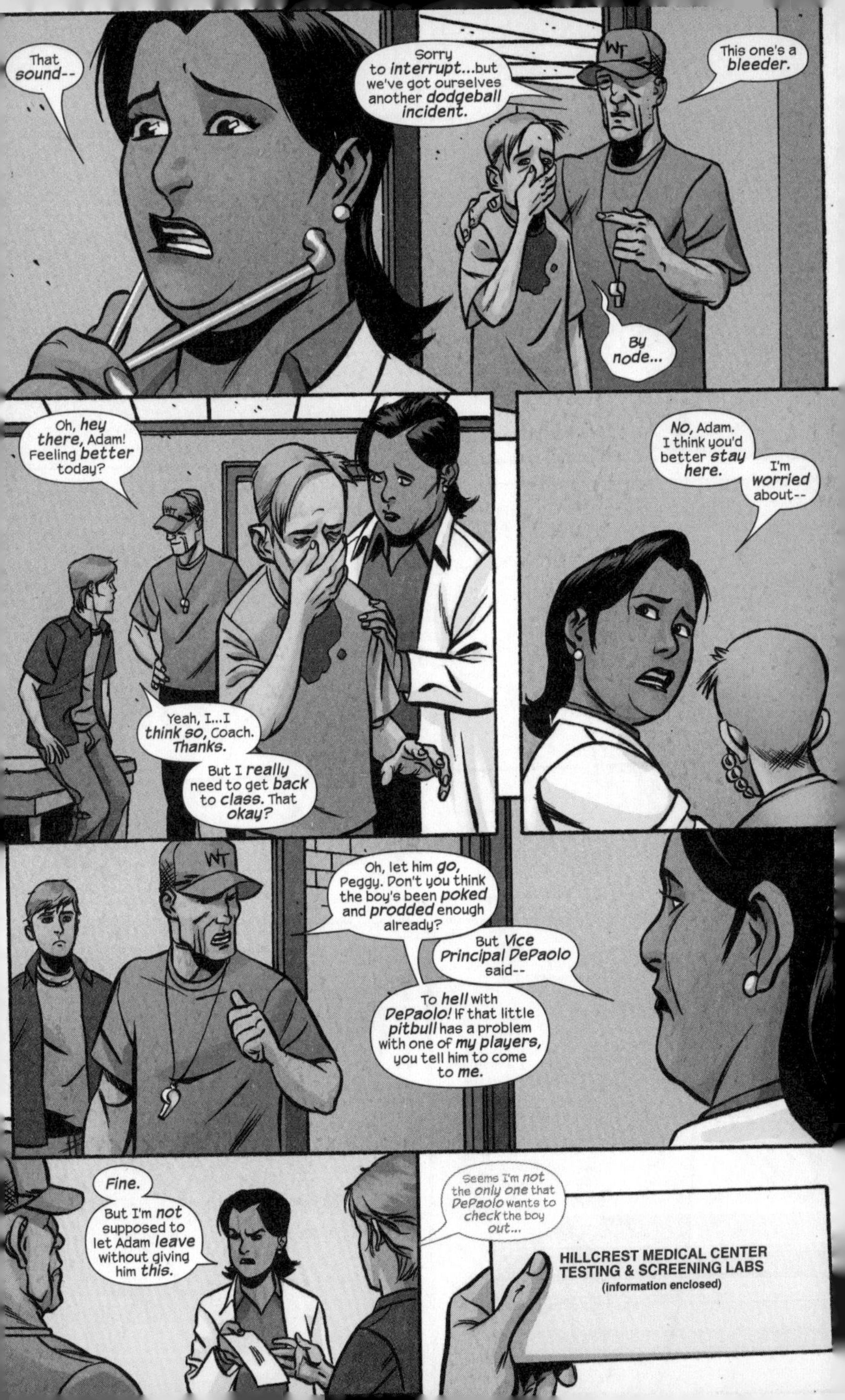

That sound--
Sorry to interrupt...but we've got ourselves another dodgeball incident.
This one's a bleeder.
By node...
Oh, hey there, Adam! Feeling better today?
Yeah, I...I think so, Coach. Thanks.
But I really need to get back to class. That okay?
No, Adam. I think you'd better stay here.
I'm worried about--
Oh, let him go, Peggy. Don't you think the boy's been poked and prodded enough already?
But Vice Principal DePaolo said--
To hell with DePaolo! If that little pitbull has a problem with one of my players, you tell him to come to me.
Fine.
But I'm not supposed to let Adam leave without giving him this.
Seems I'm not the only one that DePaolo wants to check the boy out...
HILLCREST MEDICAL CENTER
TESTING & SCREENING LABS
(information enclosed)

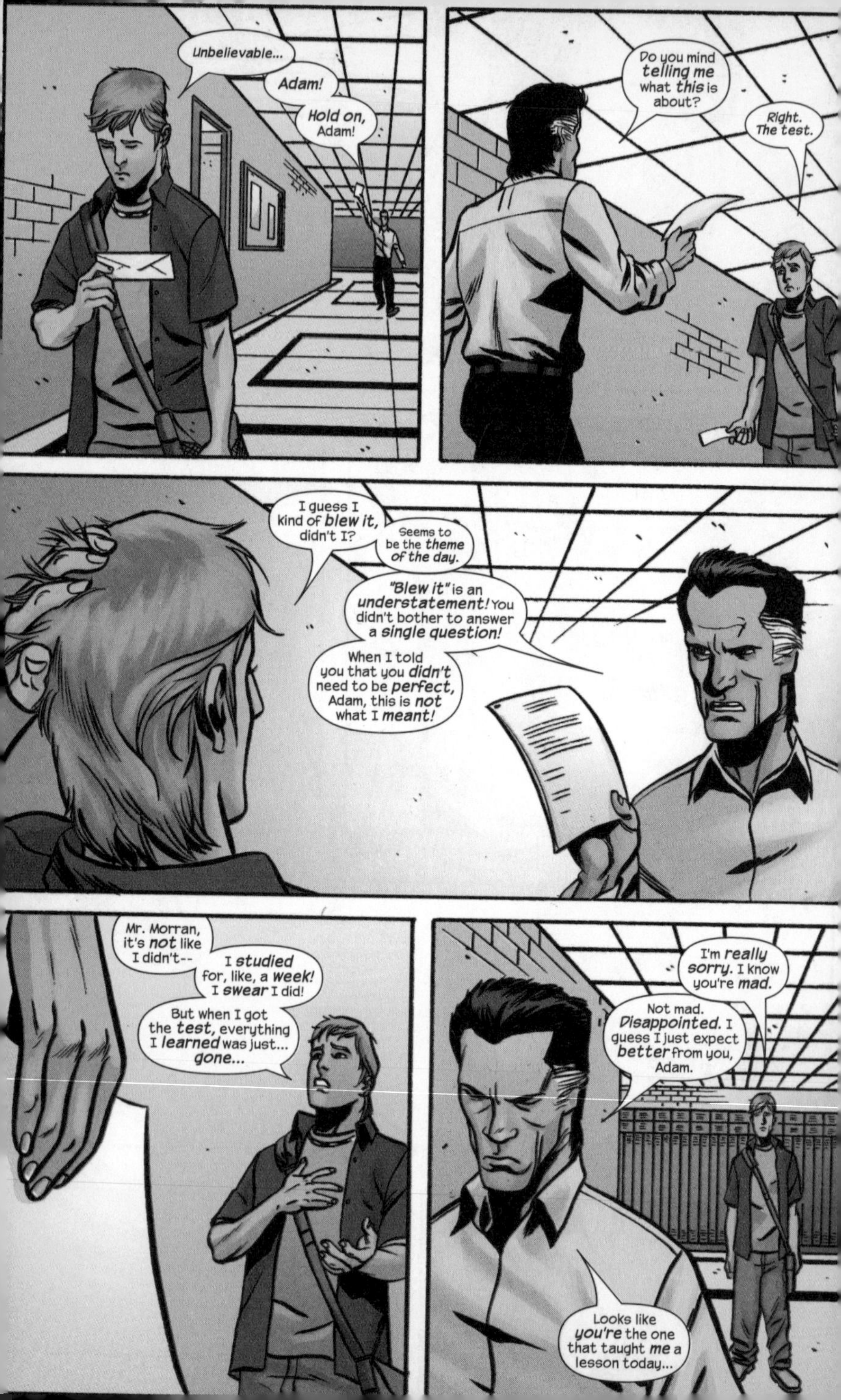
Unbelievable...
Adam!
Hold on, Adam!
Do you mind telling me what this is about?
Right. The test.
I guess I kind of blew it, didn't I?
Seems to be the theme of the day.
"Blew it" is an understatement! You didn't bother to answer a single question!
When I told you that you didn't need to be perfect, Adam, this is not what I meant!
Mr. Morran, it's not like I didn't--
I studied for, like, a week! I swear I did!
But when I got the test, everything I learned was just... gone...
I'm really sorry. I know you're mad.
Not mad. Disappointed. I guess I just expect better from you, Adam.
Looks like you're the one that taught me a lesson today...

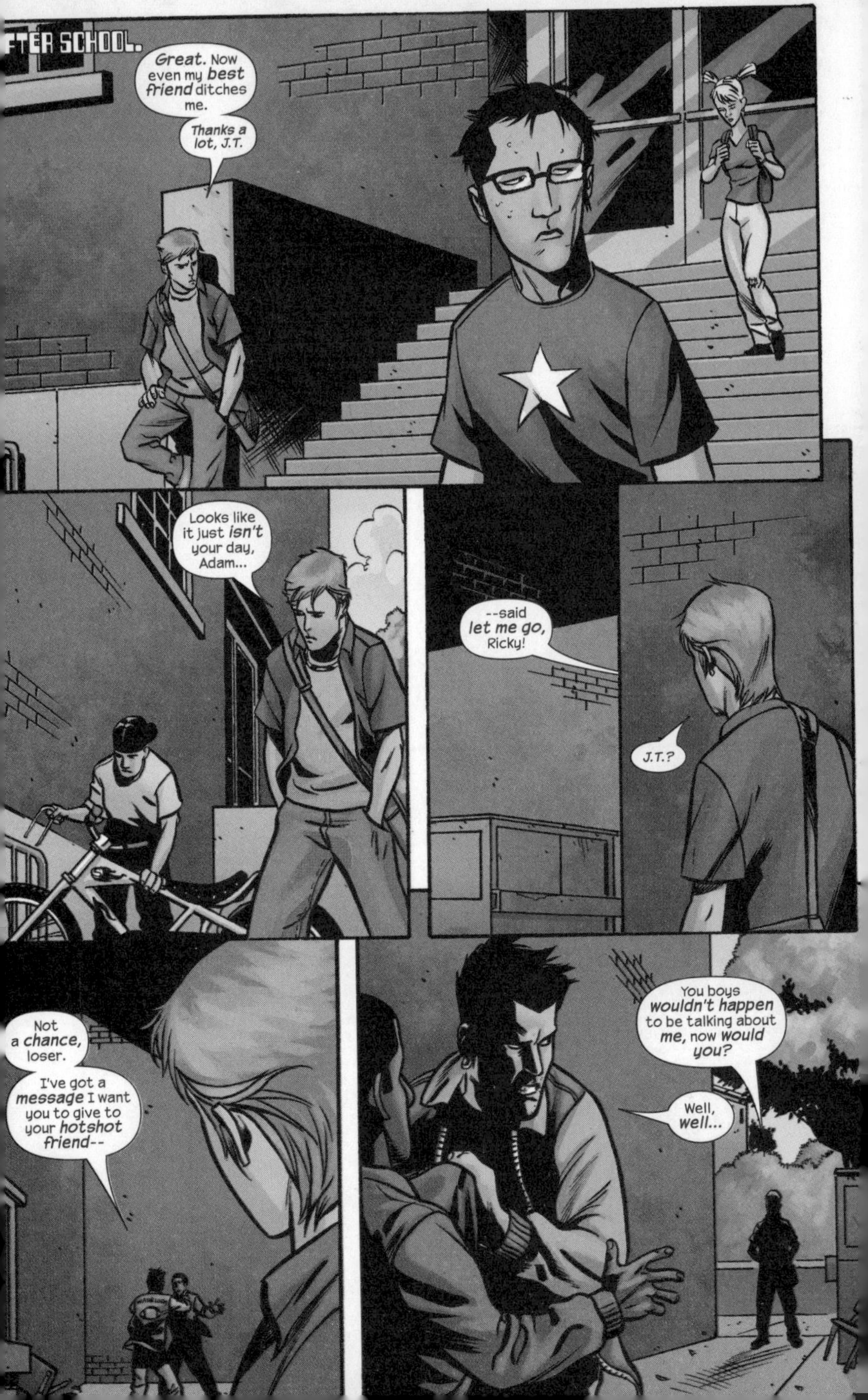

FTER SCHOOL.
Great. Now even my best friend ditches me.
Thanks a lot, J.T.
Looks like it just isn't your day, Adam...
--said let me go, Ricky!
J.T.?
Not a chance, loser.
I've got a message I want you to give to your hotshot friend--
You boys wouldn't happen to be talking about me, now would you?
Well, well...

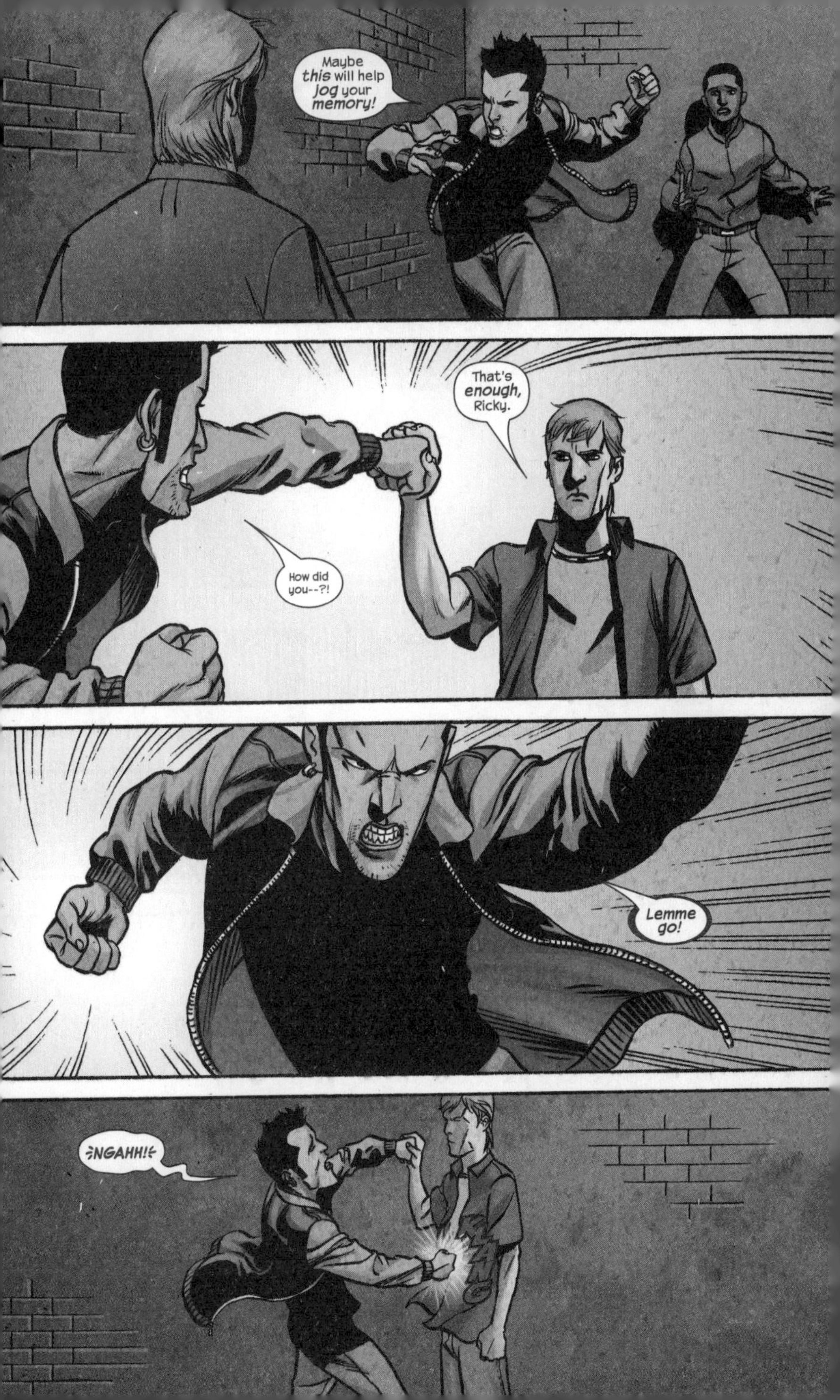
Maybe this will help jog your memory!
That's enough, Ricky.
How did you--?!
Lemme go!
NGAHH!

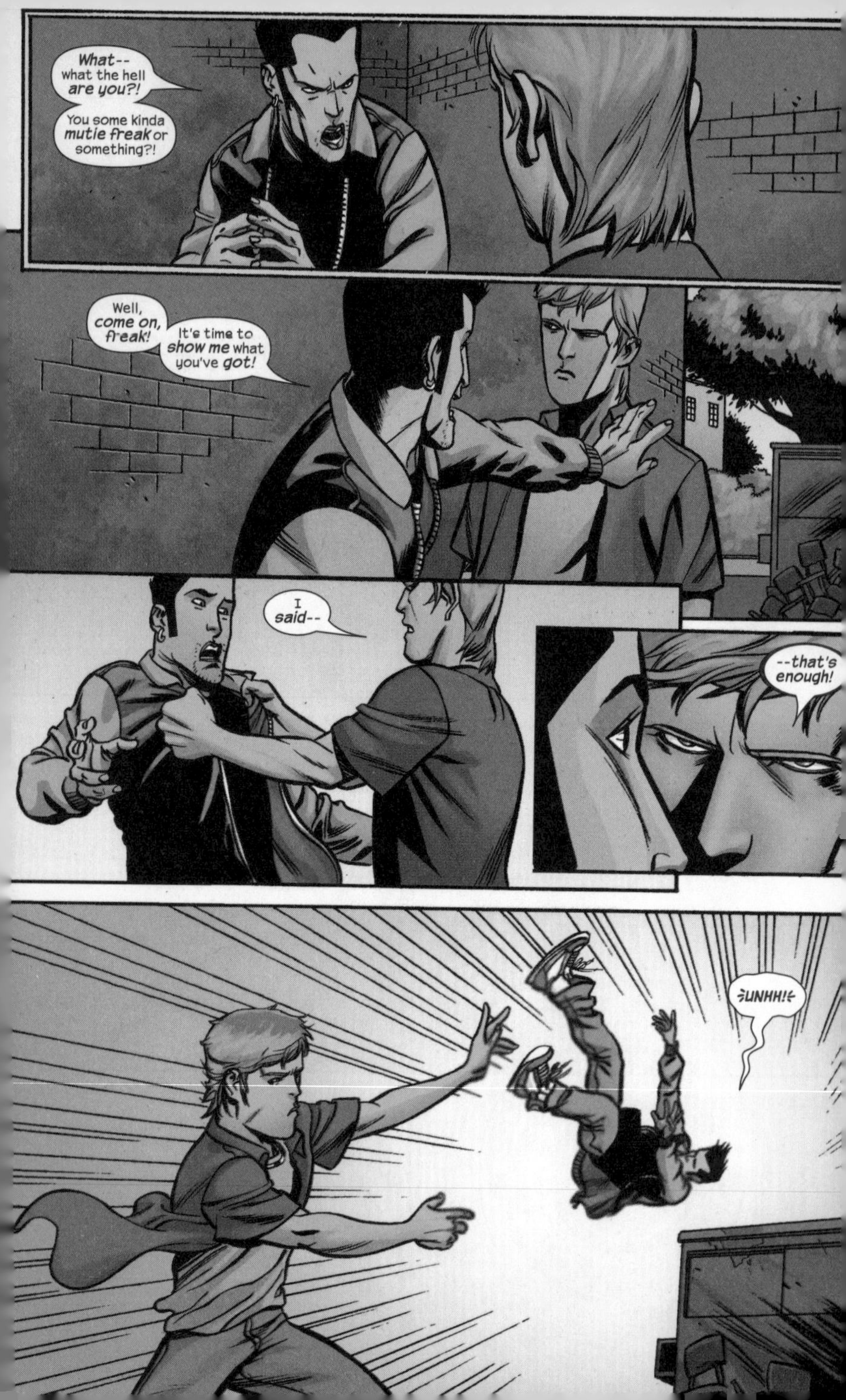
What-- what the hell are you?!
You some kinda mutie freak or something?!
Well, come on, freak!
It's time to show me what you've got!
I said--
--that's enough!
UNHH!

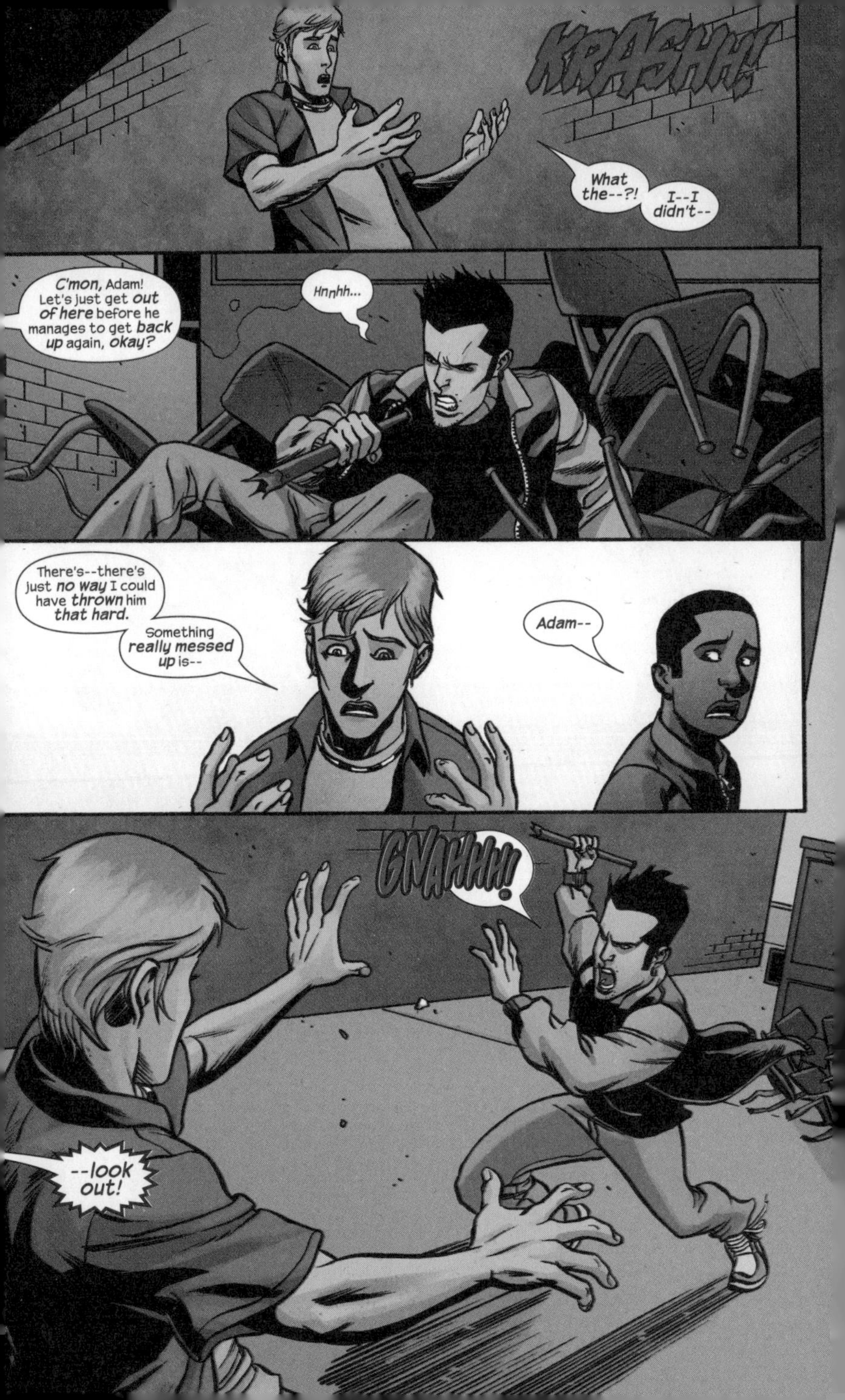

KRASHH!
What the--?!
I--I didn't--
C'mon, Adam! Let's just get out of here before he manages to get back up again, okay?
Hnnhh...
There's--there's just no way I could have thrown him that hard.
Something really messed up is--
Adam--
GNAHHHH!
--look out!

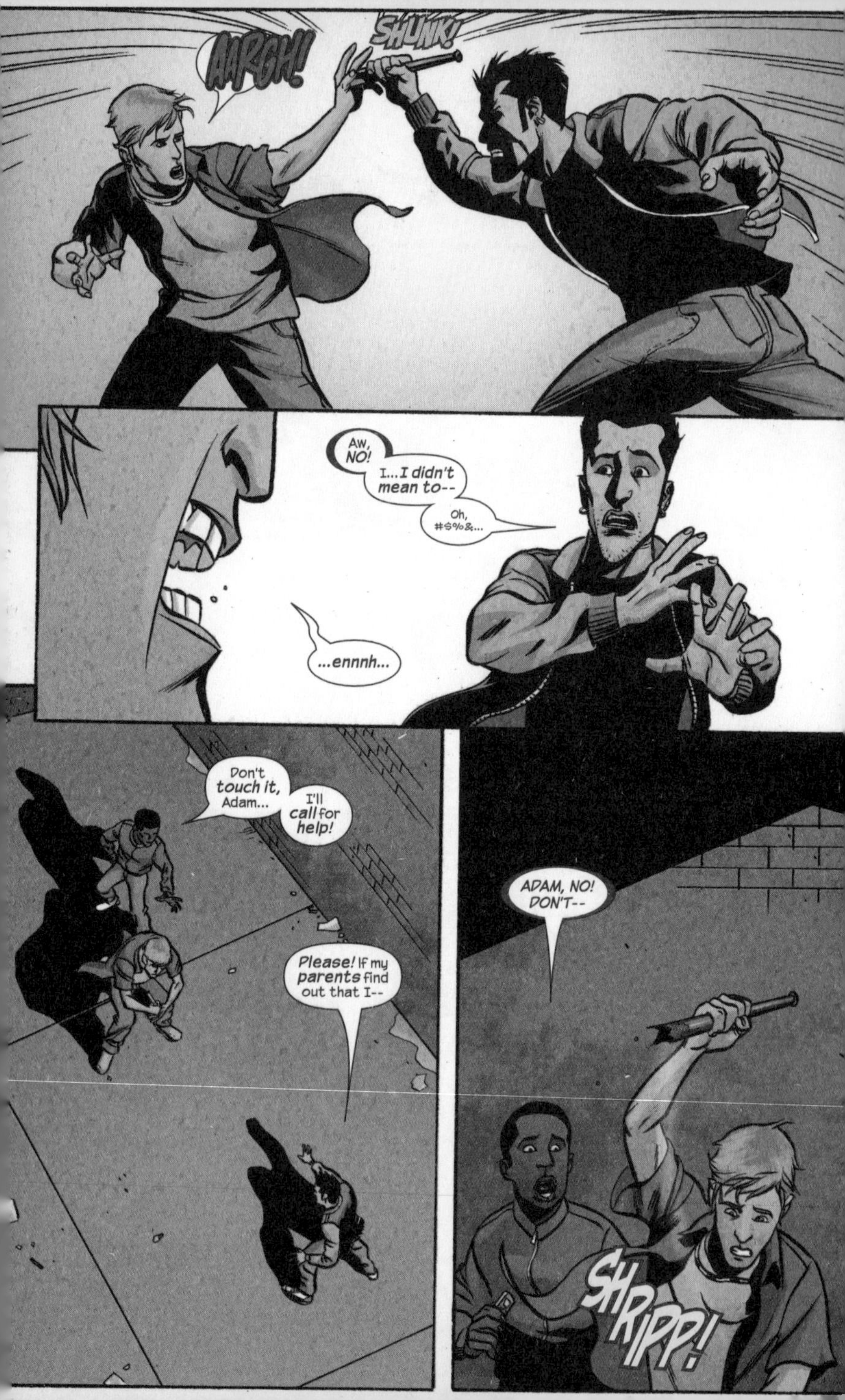

AARGH!
SHUNK!
AW, NO!
I...I didn't mean to--
Oh, #$%&...
...ennnh...
Don't touch it, Adam...
I'll call for help!
Please! If my parents find out that I--
ADAM, NO! DON'T--
SHRIPP!

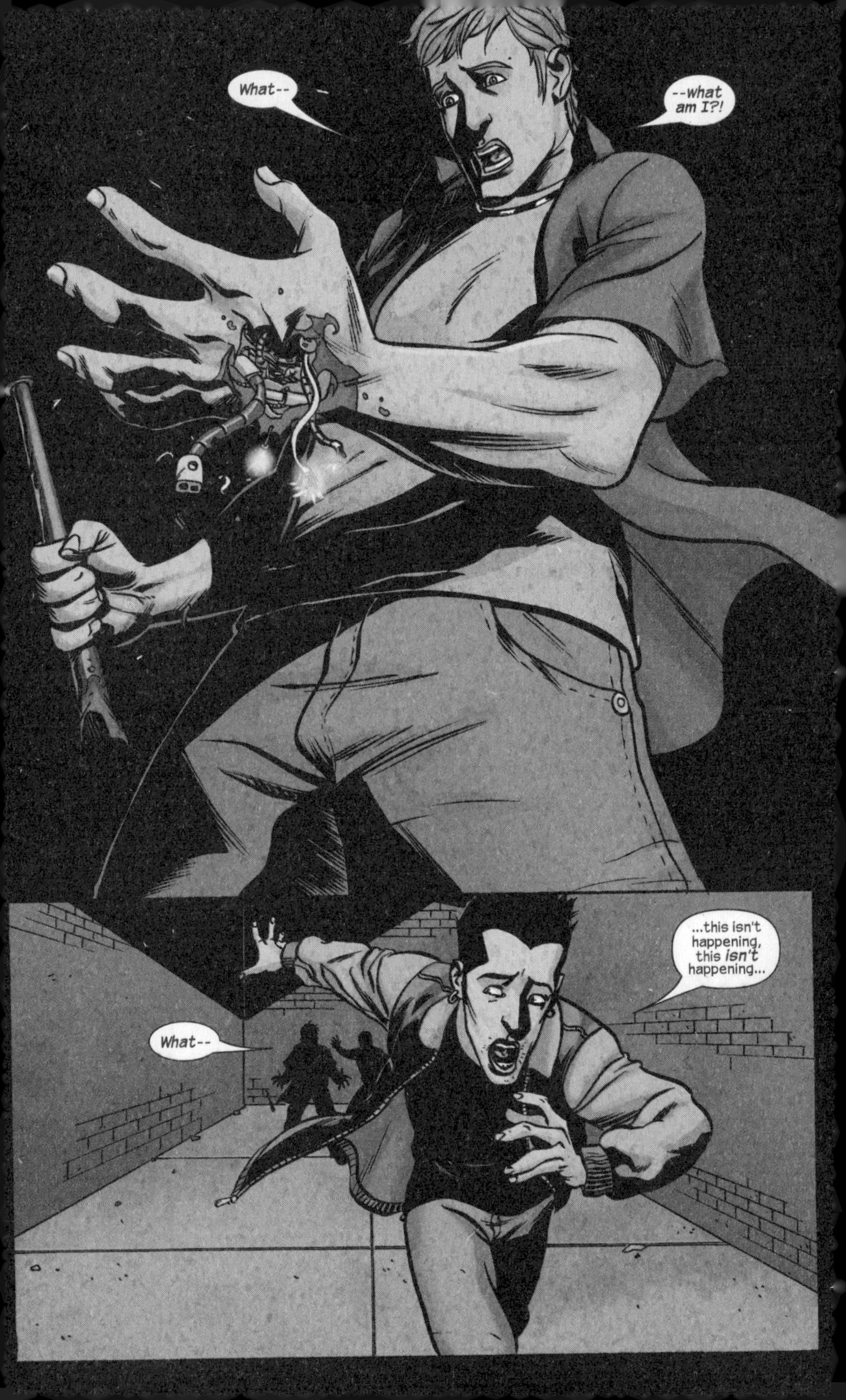
What--
--what am I?!
...this isn't happening, this *isn't* happening...
What--

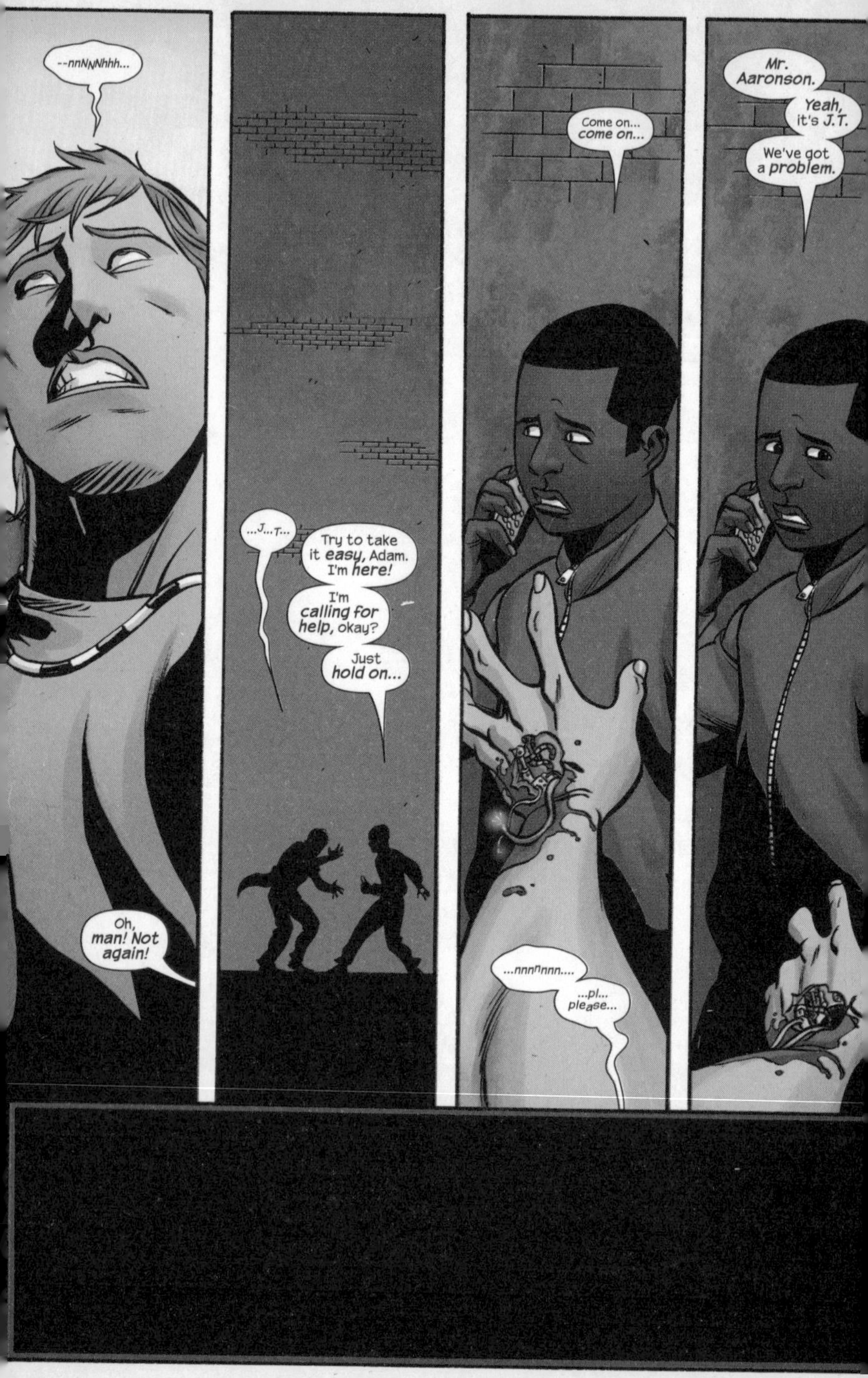
--nnNNhhh...
Oh, man! Not again!
...J...T...
Try to take it easy, Adam. I'm here!
I'm calling for help, okay?
Just hold on...
Come on... come on...
...nnnnnnn....
...pl... please...
Mr. Aaronson.
Yeah, it's J.T.
We've got a problem.

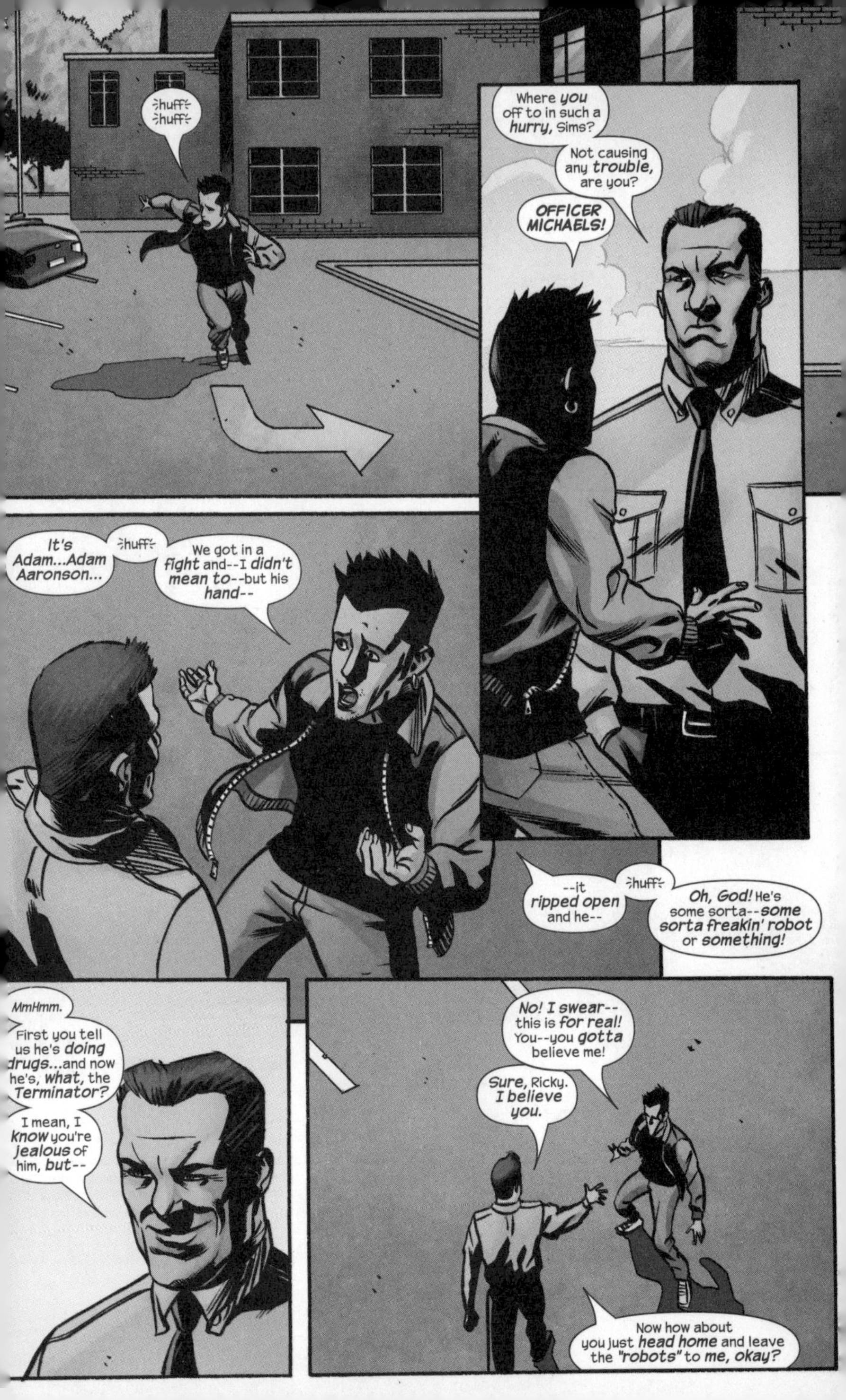

huff huff
Where you off to in such a hurry, Sims?
Not causing any trouble, are you?
OFFICER MICHAELS!
It's Adam...Adam Aaronson...
huff
We got in a fight and--I didn't mean to--but his hand--
--it ripped open and he--
huff
Oh, God! He's some sorta--some sorta freakin' robot or something!
MmHmm.
First you tell us he's doing drugs...and now he's, what, the Terminator?
I mean, I know you're jealous of him, but--
No! I swear--this is for real! You--you gotta believe me!
Sure, Ricky. I believe you.
Now how about you just head home and leave the "robots" to me, okay?

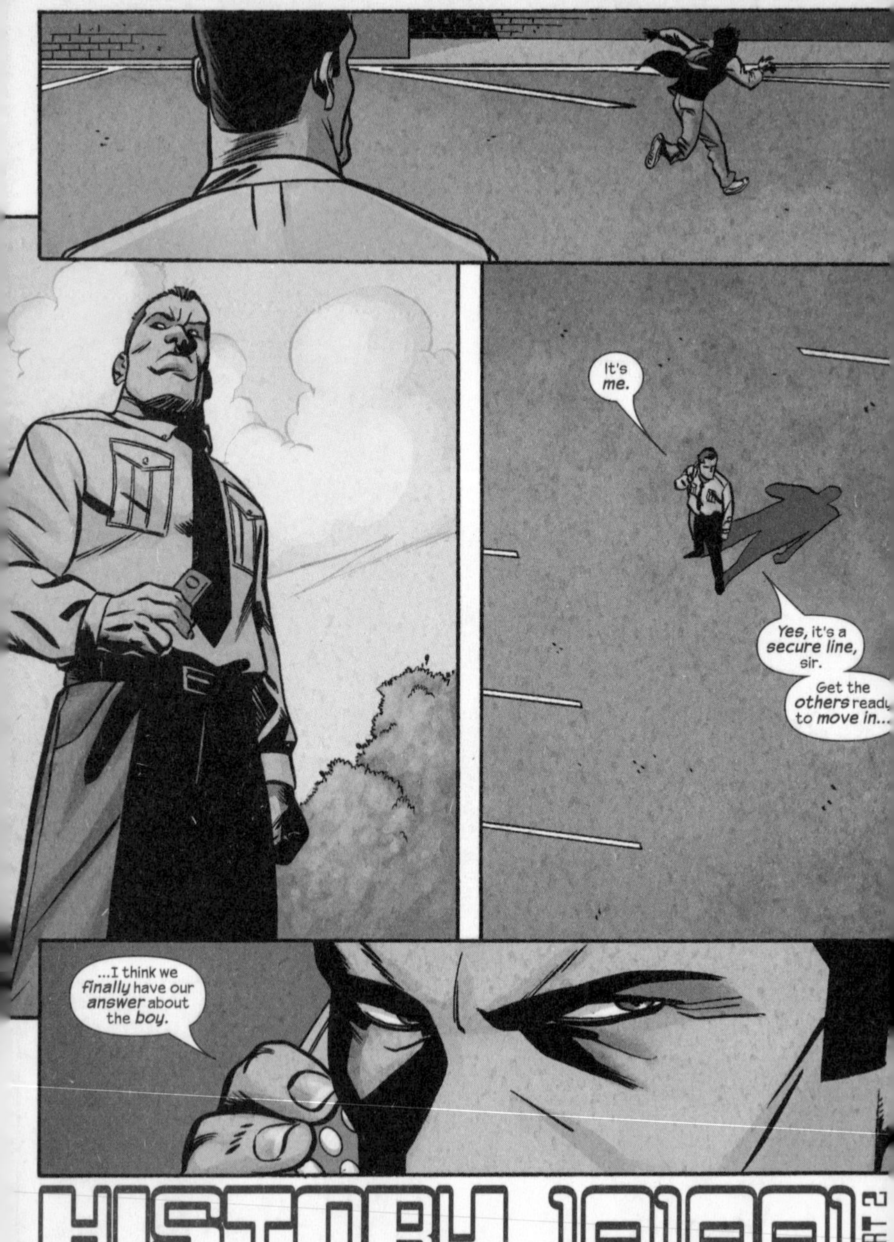
It's me.
Yes, it's a secure line, sir.
Get the others ready to move in...
...I think we finally have our answer about the boy.

HISTORY 101001 PART 2

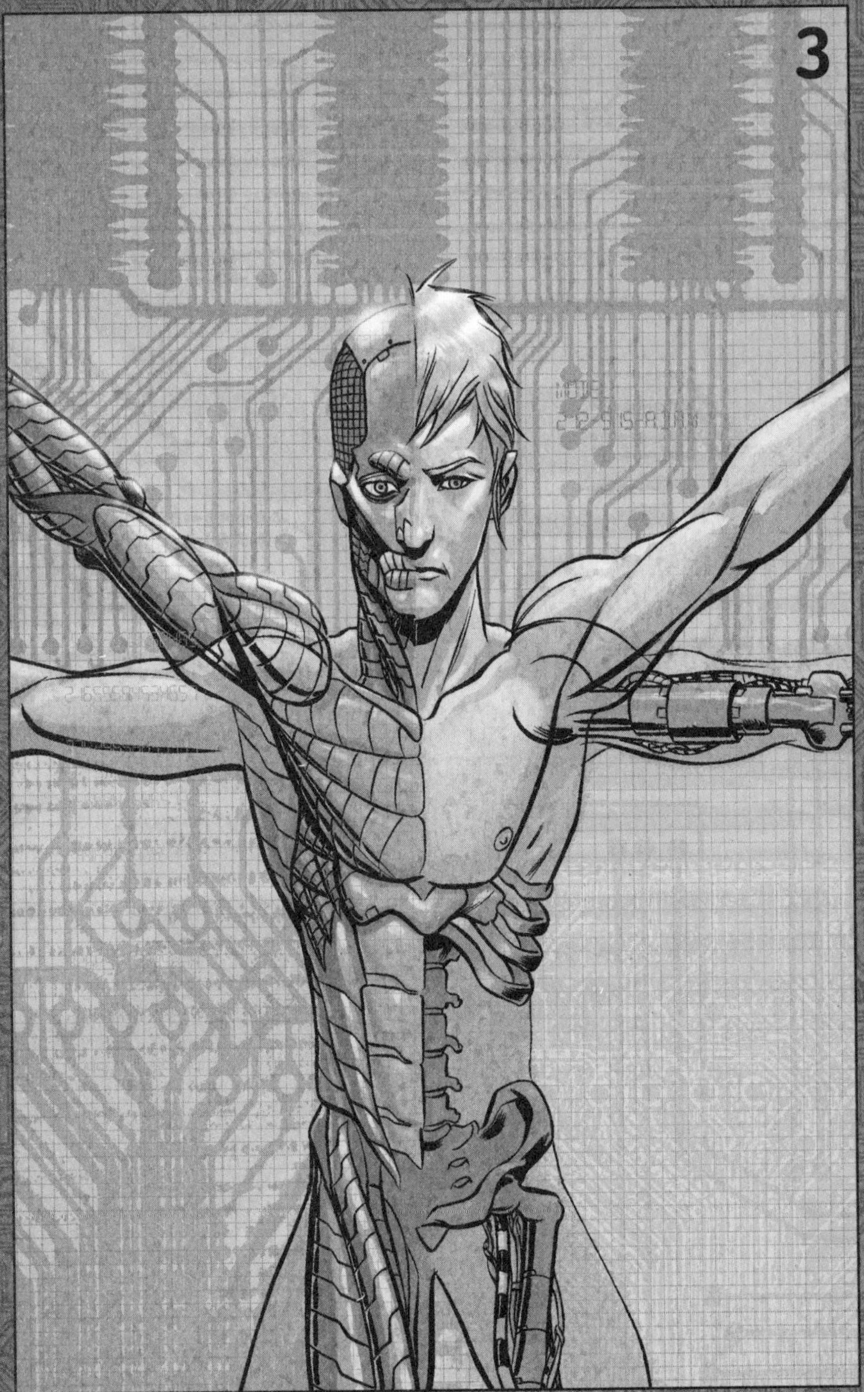
3

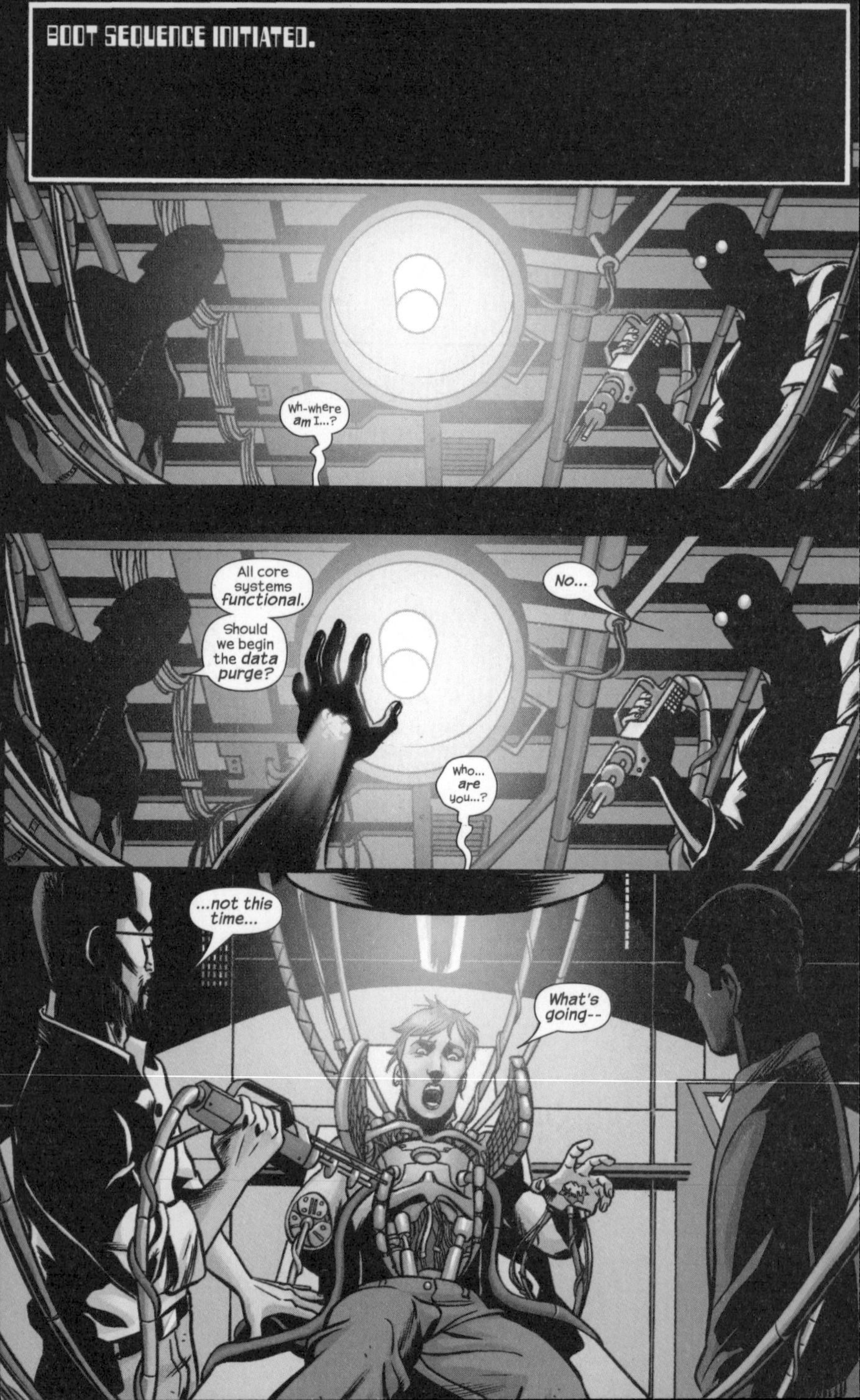
BOOT SEQUENCE INITIATED.
Wh-where am I...?
All core systems functional.
Should we begin the data purge?
No...
Who... are you...?
...not this time...
What's going--

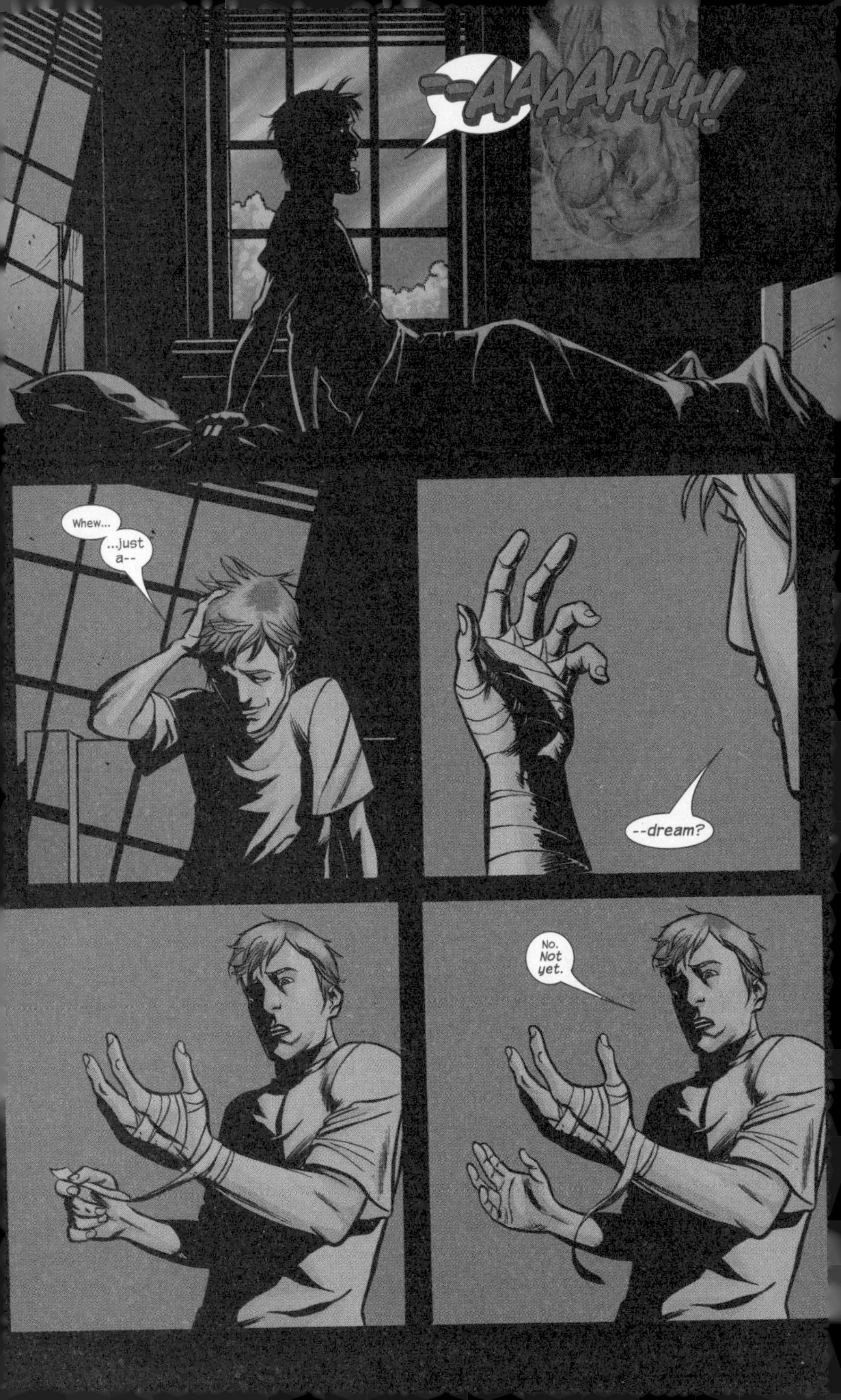
--AAAAHHH!
Whew...
...just a--
--dream?
No. Not yet.

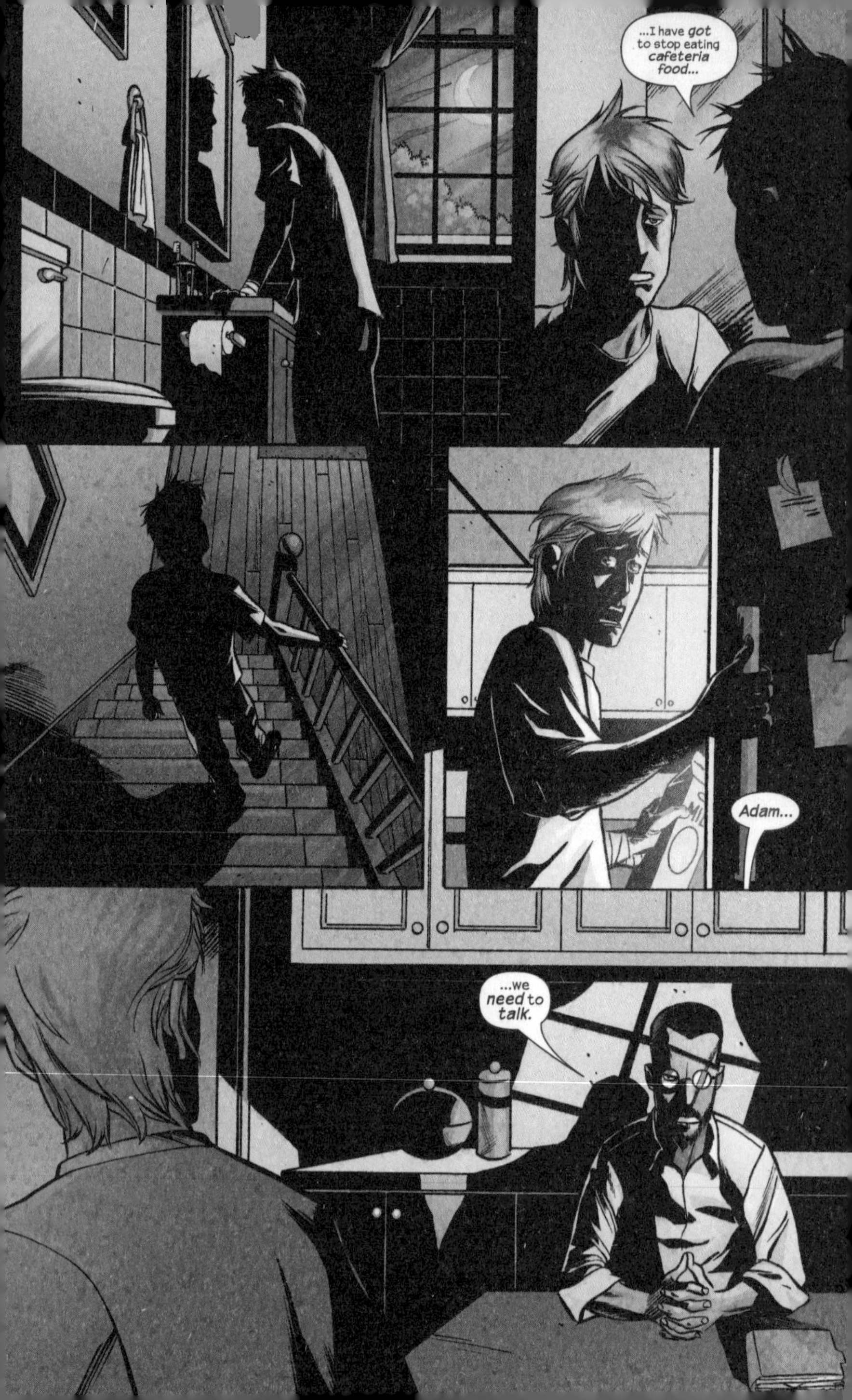
...I have got to stop eating cafeteria food...
Adam...
...we need to talk.

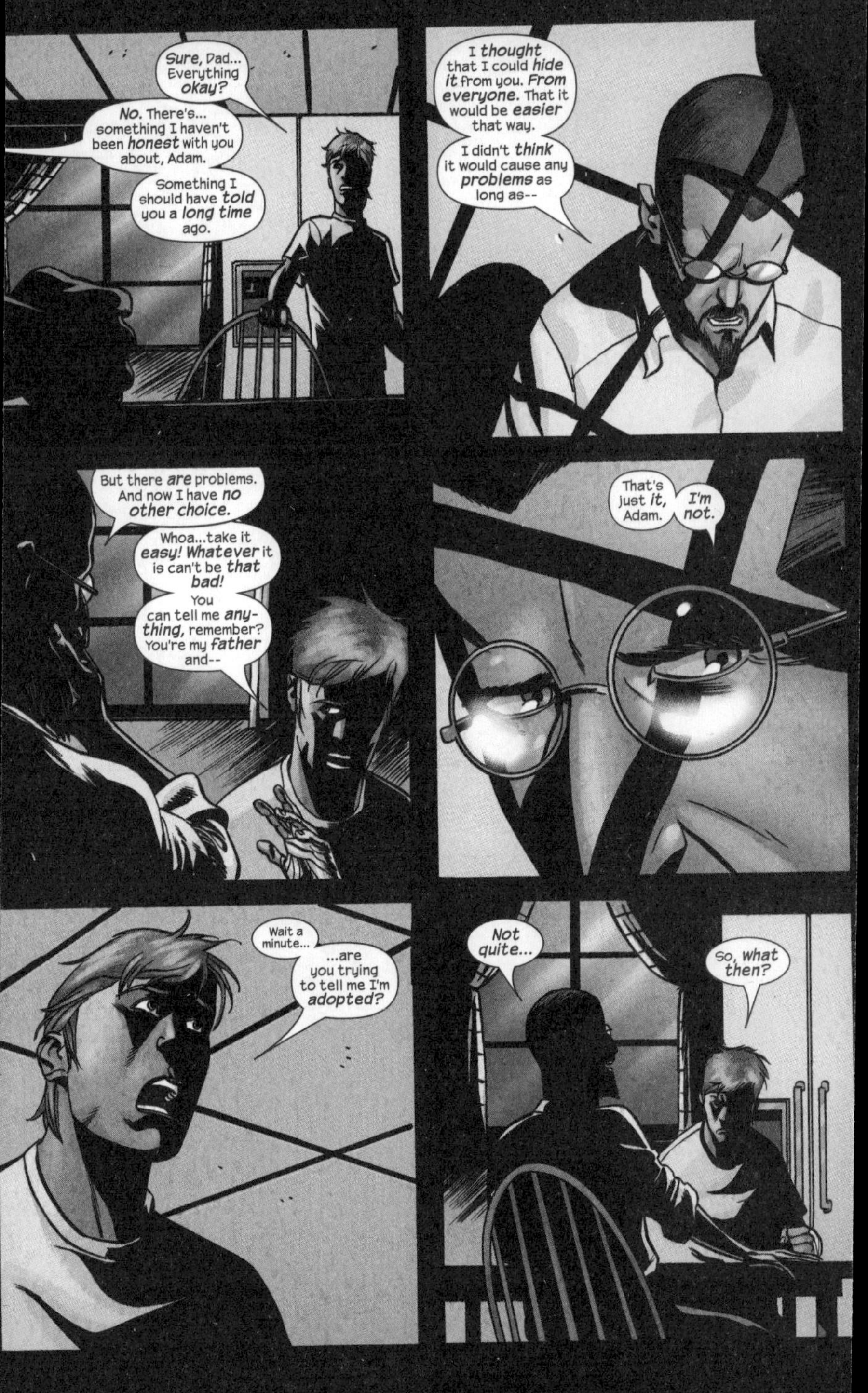
Sure, Dad... Everything okay?
No. There's... something I haven't been honest with you about, Adam.
Something I should have told you a long time ago.
I thought that I could hide it from you. From everyone. That it would be easier that way.
I didn't think it would cause any problems as long as--
But there are problems. And now I have no other choice.
Whoa...take it easy! Whatever it is can't be that bad!
You can tell me any-thing, remember? You're my father and--
That's just it, Adam.
I'm not.
Wait a minute...
...are you trying to tell me I'm adopted?
Not quite...
So, what then?

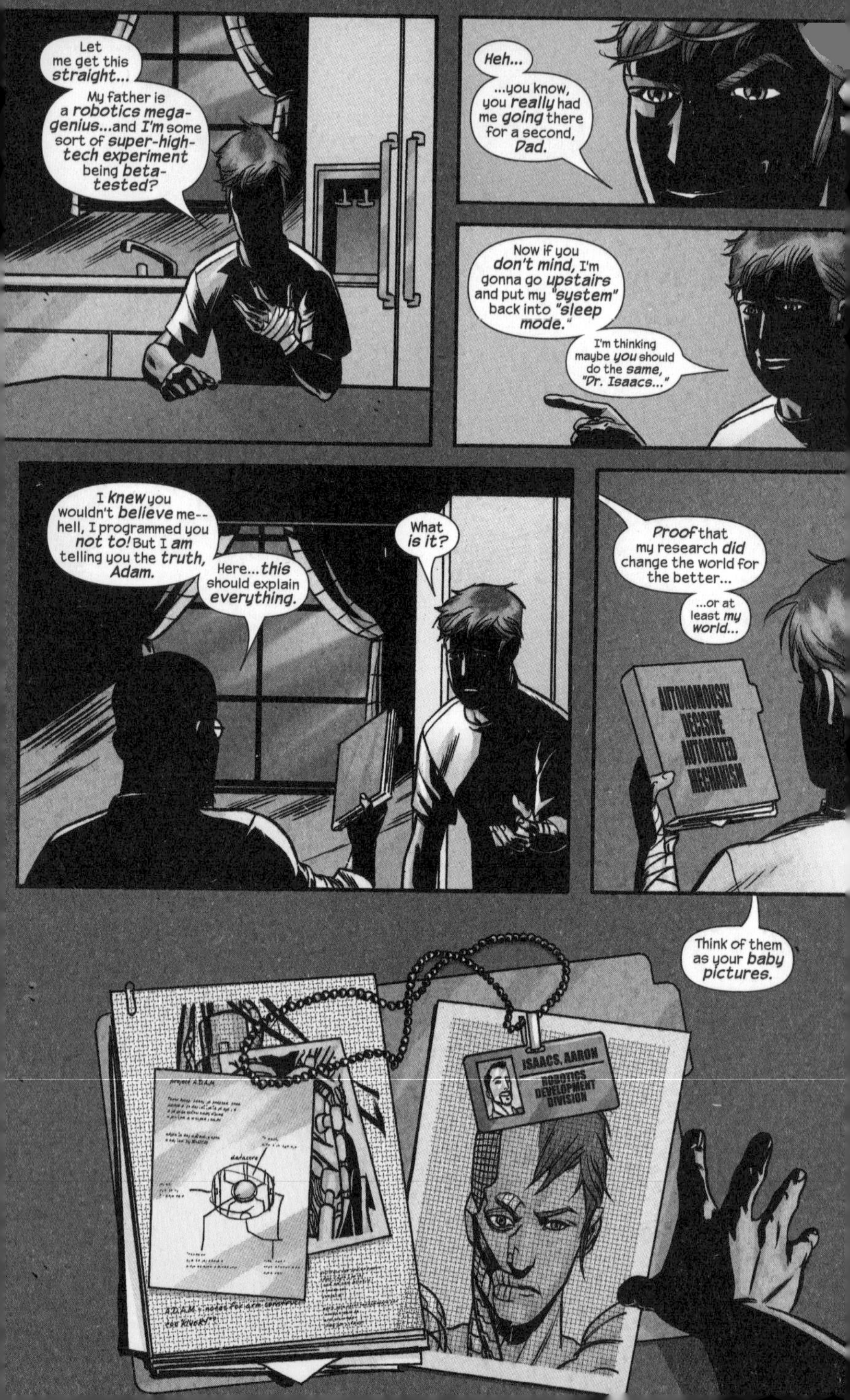
Let me get this straight...
My father is a robotics mega-genius...and I'm some sort of super-high-tech experiment being beta-tested?
Heh...
...you know, you really had me going there for a second, Dad.
Now if you don't mind, I'm gonna go upstairs and put my "system" back into "sleep mode."
I'm thinking maybe you should do the same, "Dr. Isaacs..."
I knew you wouldn't believe me--hell, I programmed you not to! But I am telling you the truth, Adam.
Here...this should explain everything.
What is it?
Proof that my research did change the world for the better...
...or at least my world...
AUTONOMOUSLY DECISIVE AUTOMATED MECHANISM
Think of them as your baby pictures.
ISAACS, AARON
ROBOTICS DEVELOPMENT DIVISION

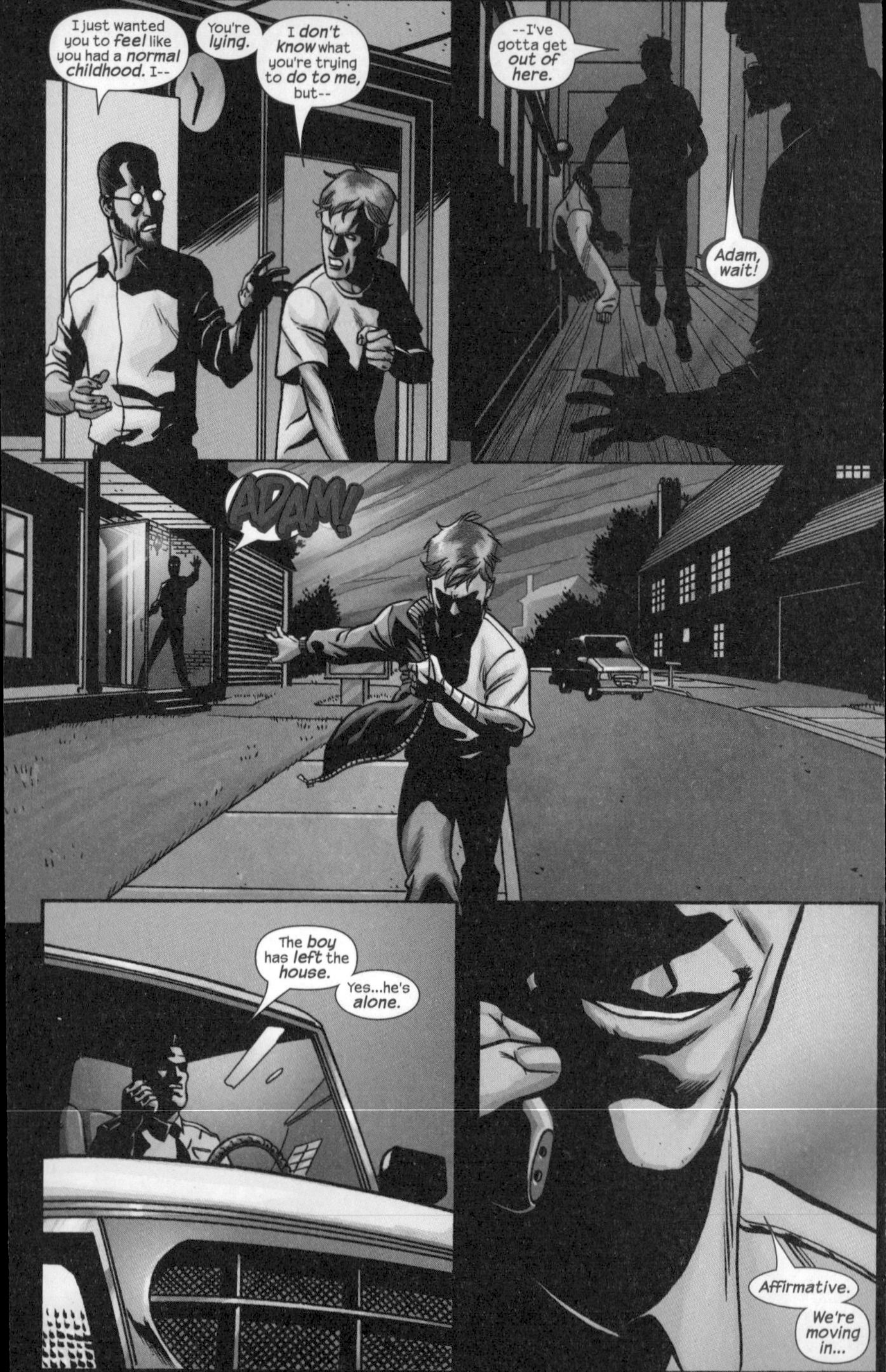
I just wanted you to feel like you had a normal childhood. I--
You're lying.
I don't know what you're trying to do to me, but--
--I've gotta get out of here.
Adam, wait!
ADAM!
The boy has left the house.
Yes...he's alone.
Affirmative.
We're moving in...

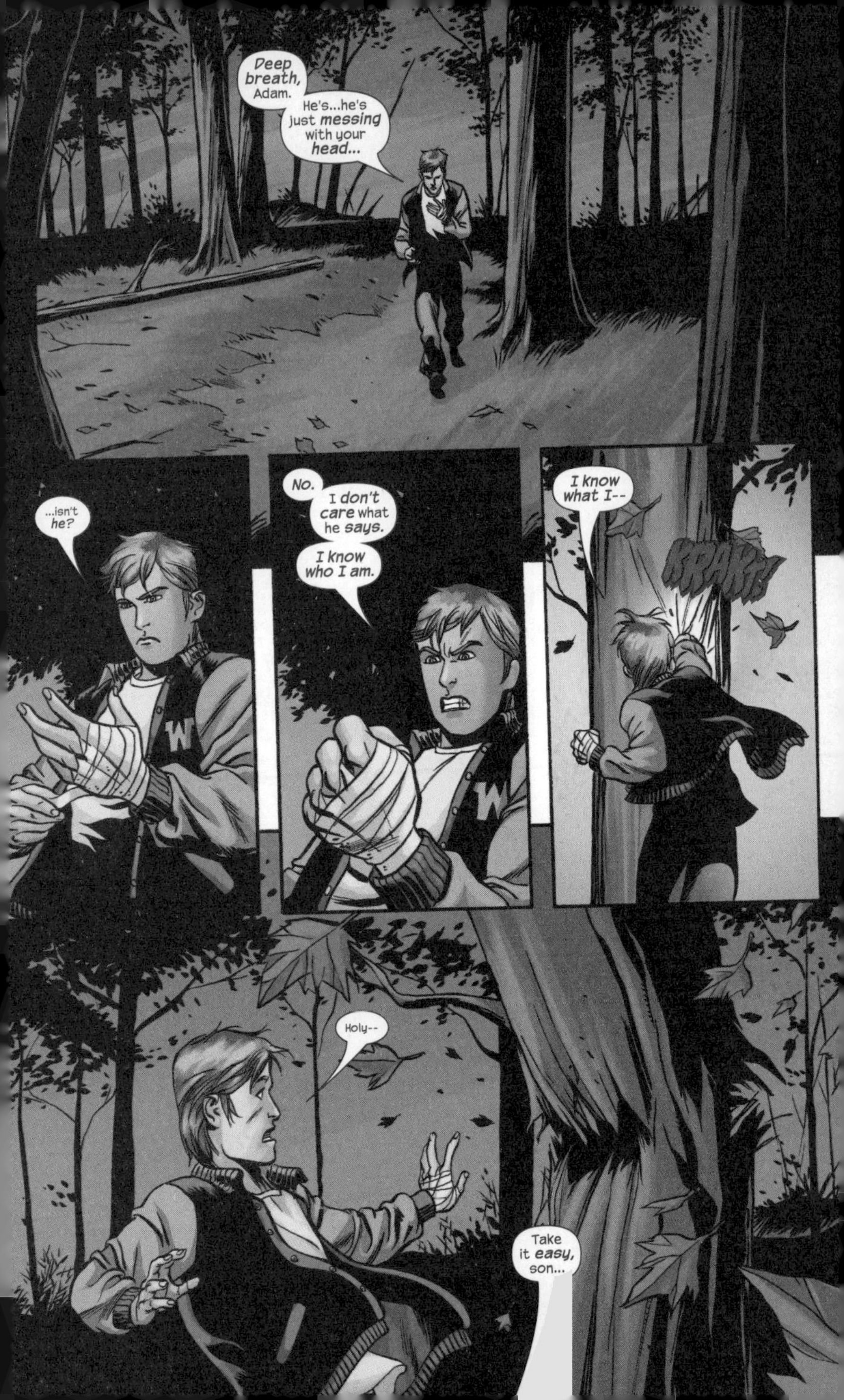
Deep breath, Adam.
He's...he's just messing with your head...
...isn't he?
No.
I don't care what he says.
I know who I am.
I know what I--
Holy--
Take it easy, son...

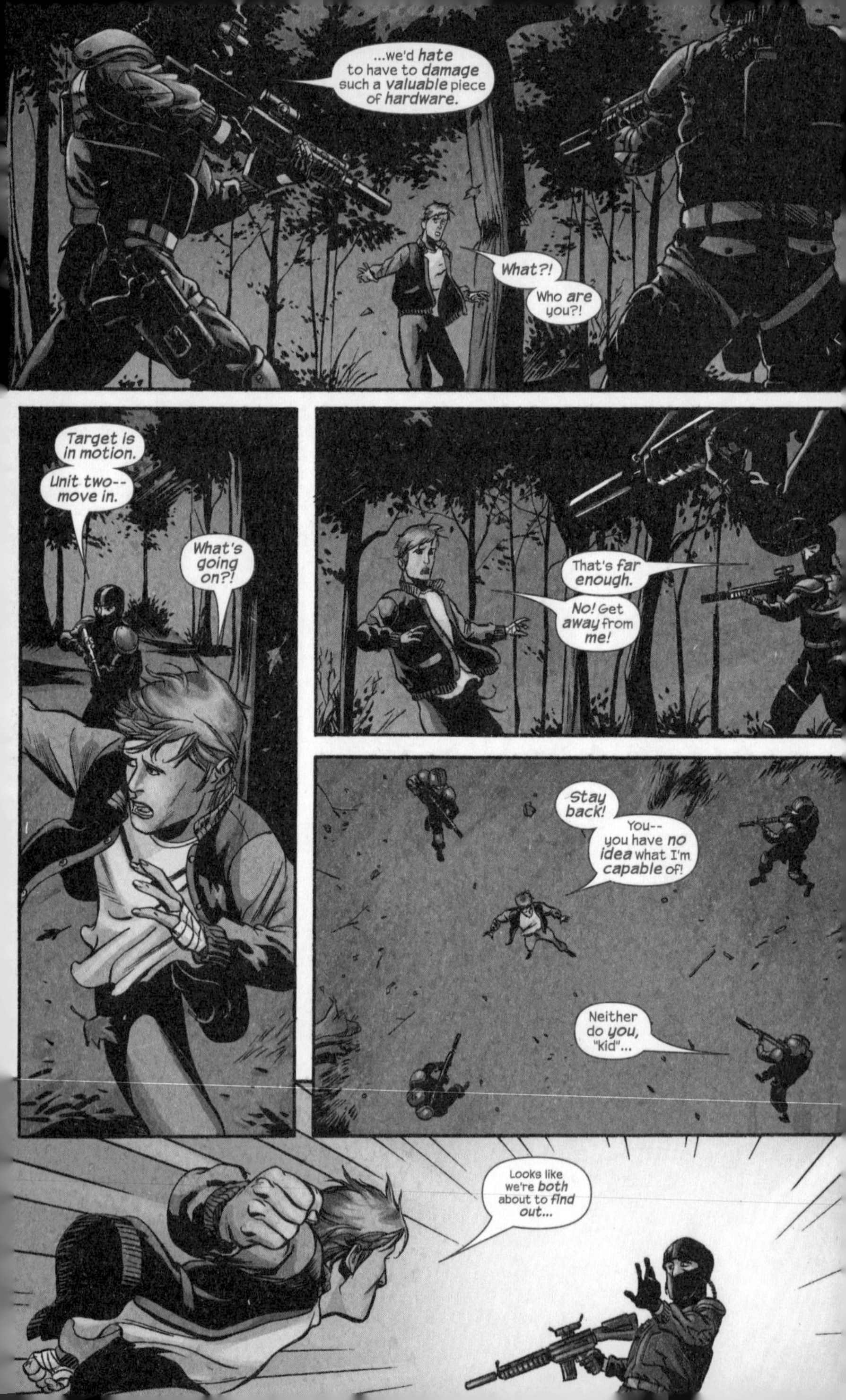
...we'd hate to have to damage such a valuable piece of hardware.
What?!
Who are you?!
Target is in motion.
Unit two-- move in.
What's going on?!
That's far enough.
No! Get away from me!
Stay back!
You-- you have no idea what I'm capable of!
Neither do you, "kid"...
Looks like we're both about to find out...

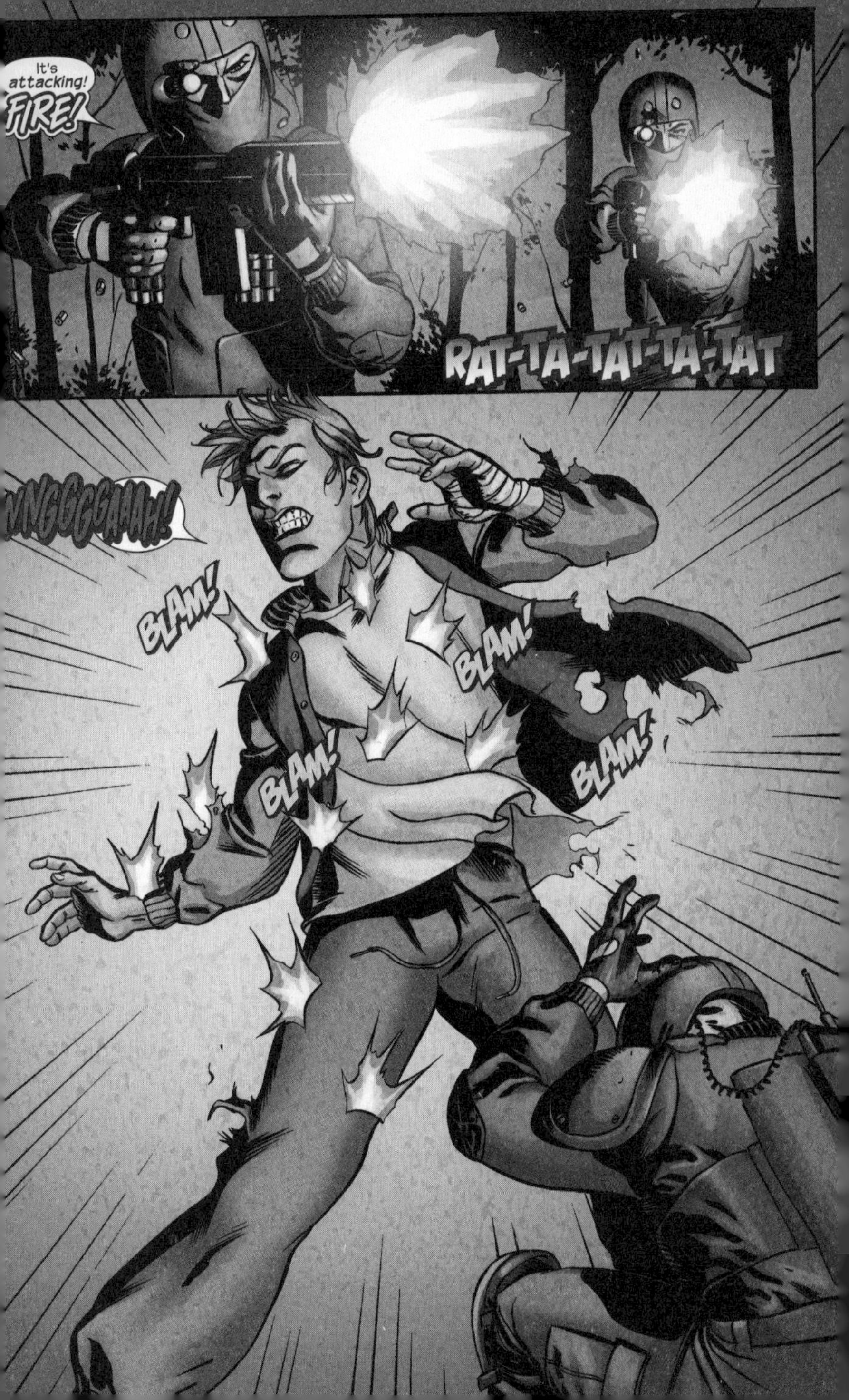

It's attacking! FIRE!
RAT-TA-TAT-TA-TAT
NNGGGAAAH!
BLAM!
BLAM!
BLAM!
BLAM!

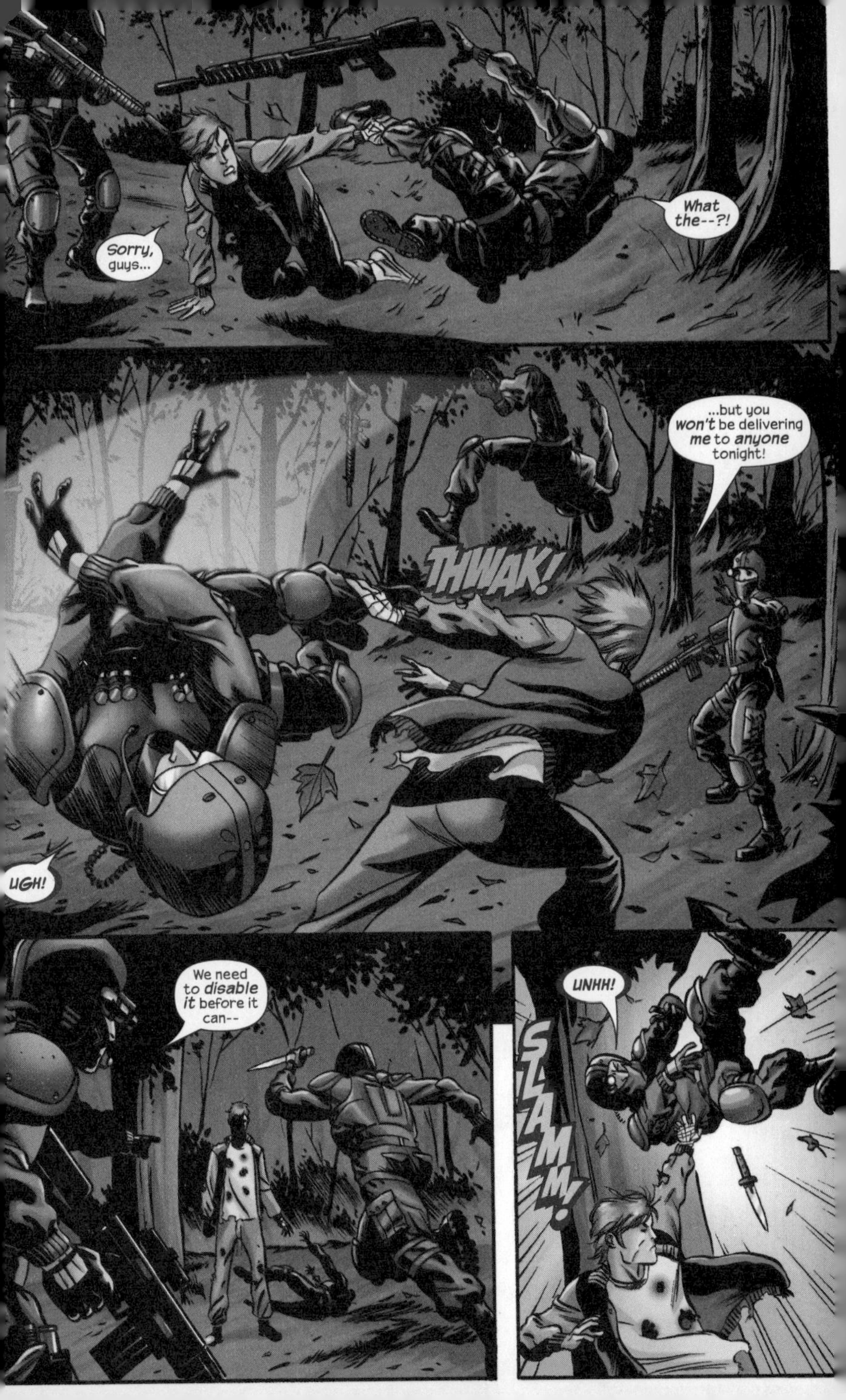
Sorry, guys...
What the--?!
...but you won't be delivering me to anyone tonight!
THWAK!
UGH!
We need to disable it before it can--
UNHH!
SLAMM!

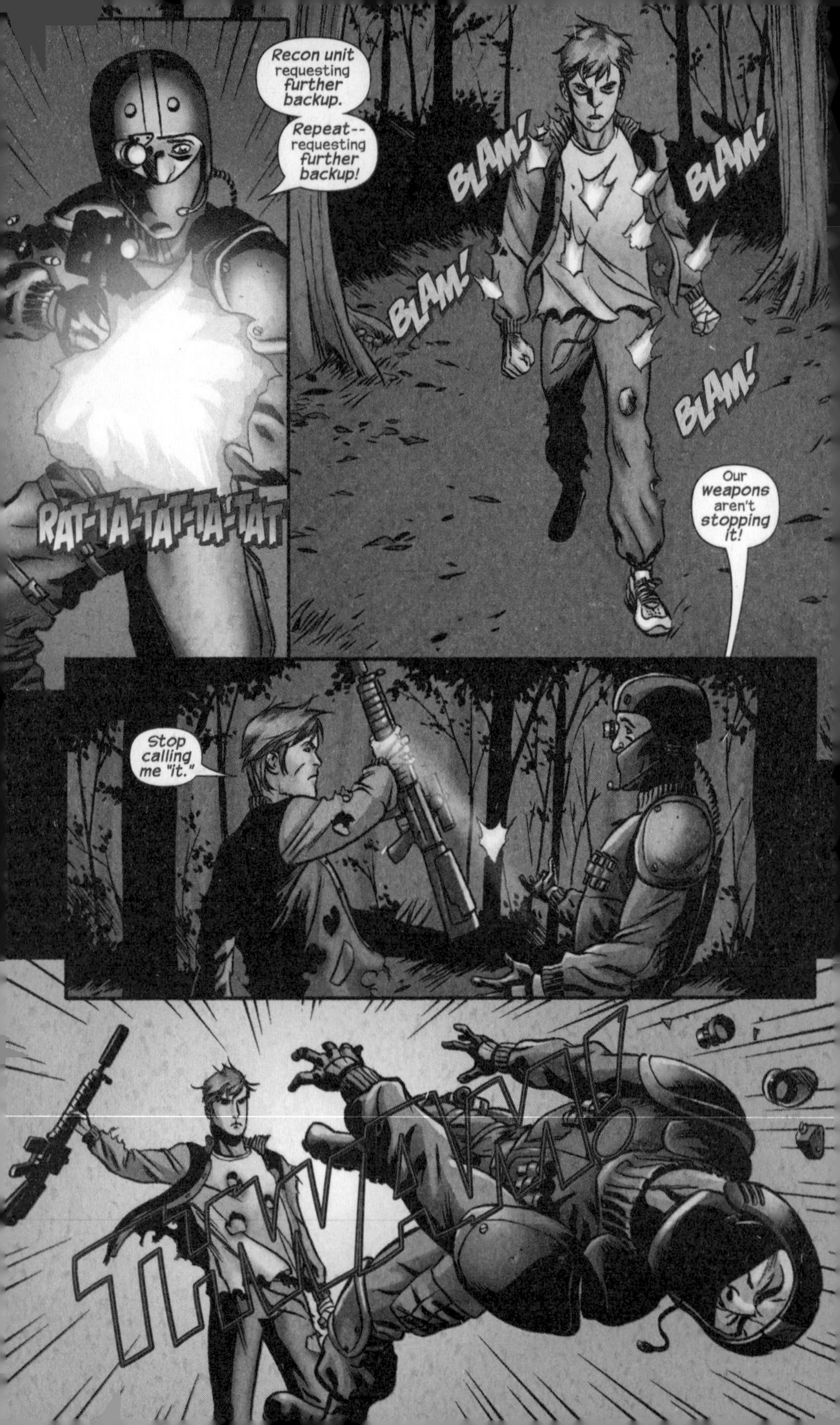
Recon unit requesting further backup.
Repeat-- requesting further backup!
RAT-TA-TAT-TA-TAT
BLAM!
BLAM!
BLAM!
BLAM!
Our weapons aren't stopping it!
Stop calling me "it."

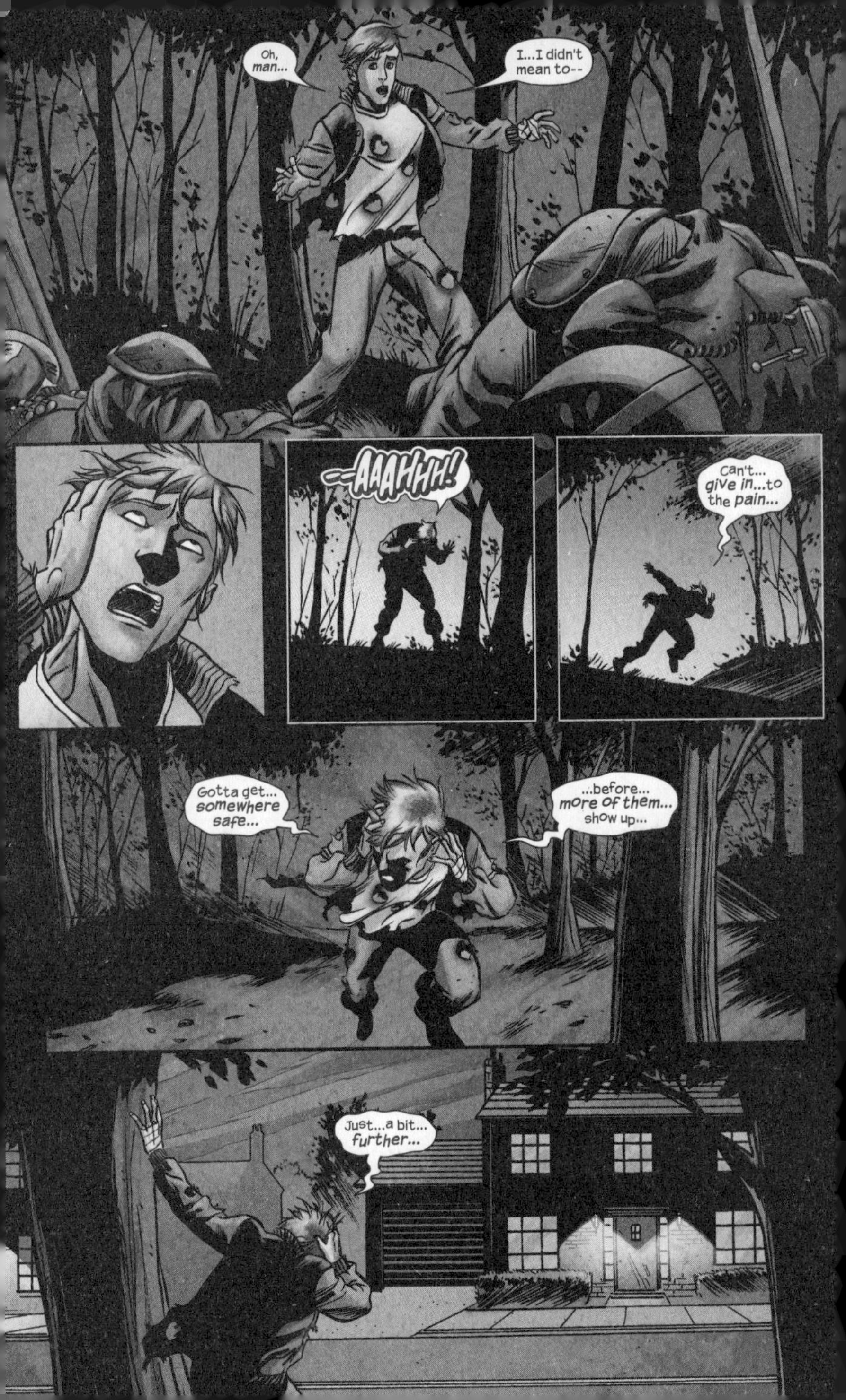
Oh, man...
I...I didn't mean to--
--AAAHHH!
Can't... give in...to the pain...
Gotta get... somewhere safe...
...before... more of them... show up...
Just...a bit... further...

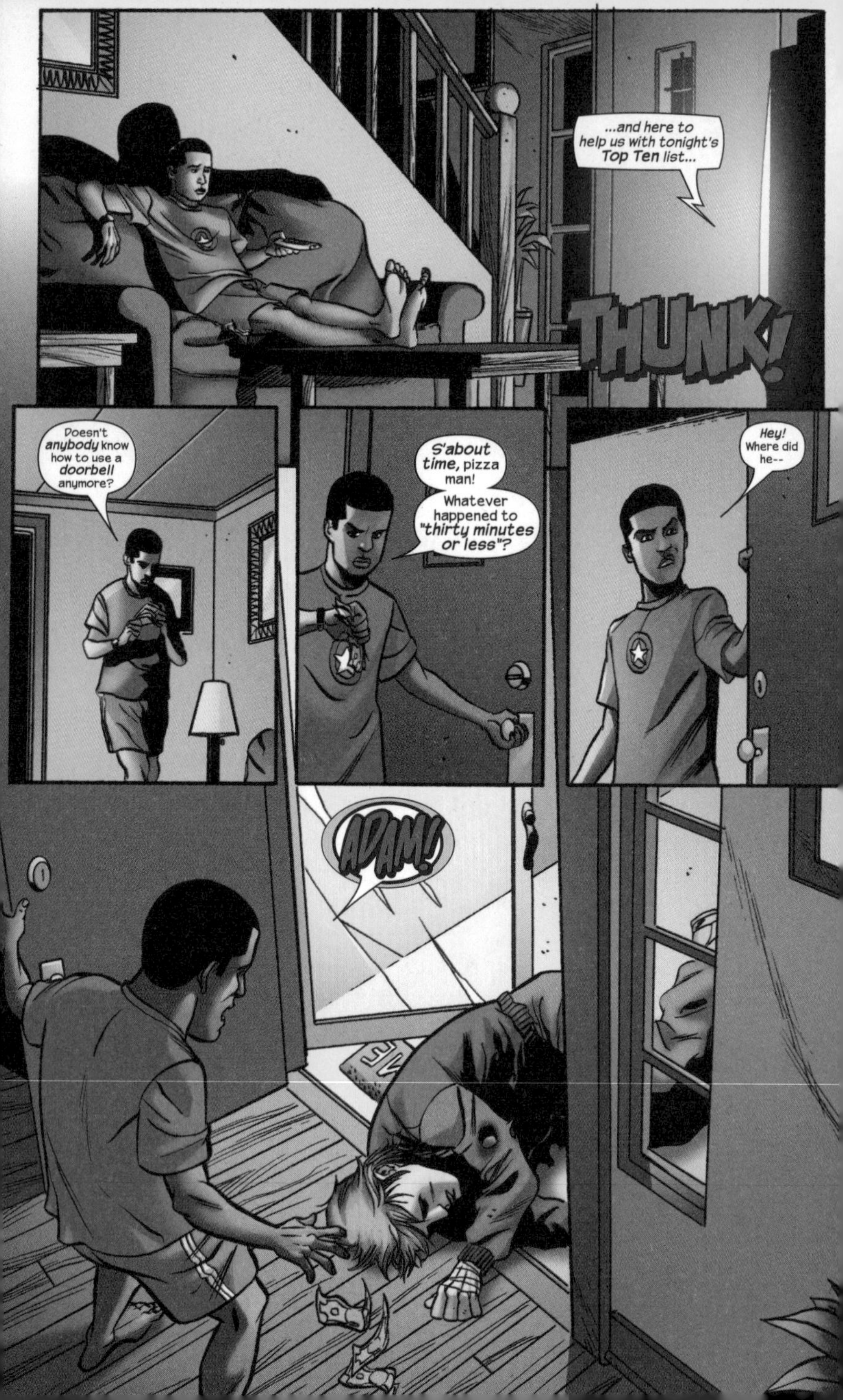
...and here to help us with tonight's Top Ten list...
THUNK!
Doesn't anybody know how to use a doorbell anymore?
S'about time, pizza man!
Whatever happened to "thirty minutes or less"?
Hey! Where did he--
ADAM!

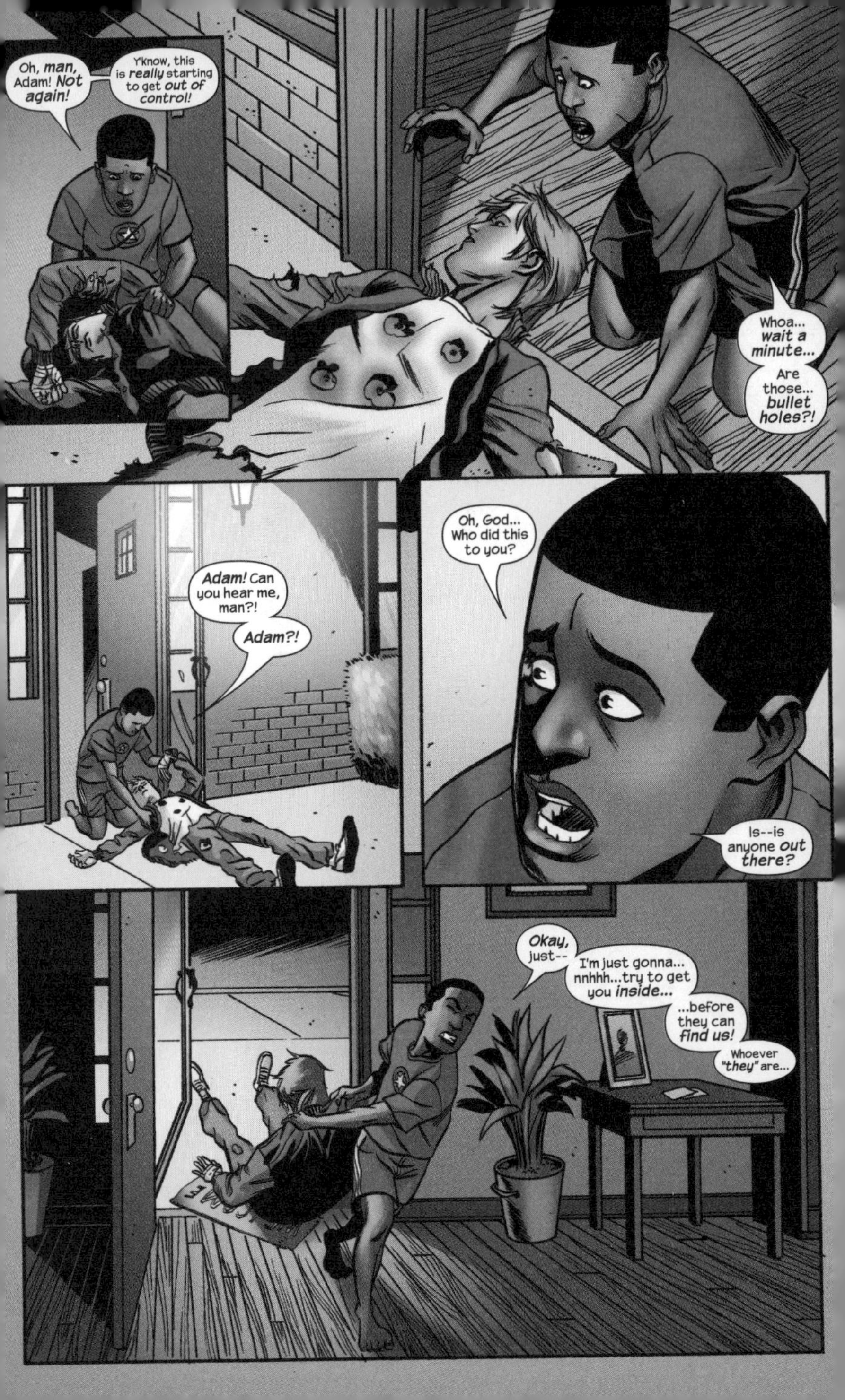
Oh, man, Adam! Not again!
Y'know, this is really starting to get out of control!
Whoa... wait a minute...
Are those... bullet holes?!
Adam! Can you hear me, man?!
Adam?!
Oh, God... Who did this to you?
Is--is anyone out there?
Okay, just--
I'm just gonna... nnhhh...try to get you inside...
...before they can find us!
Whoever "they" are...

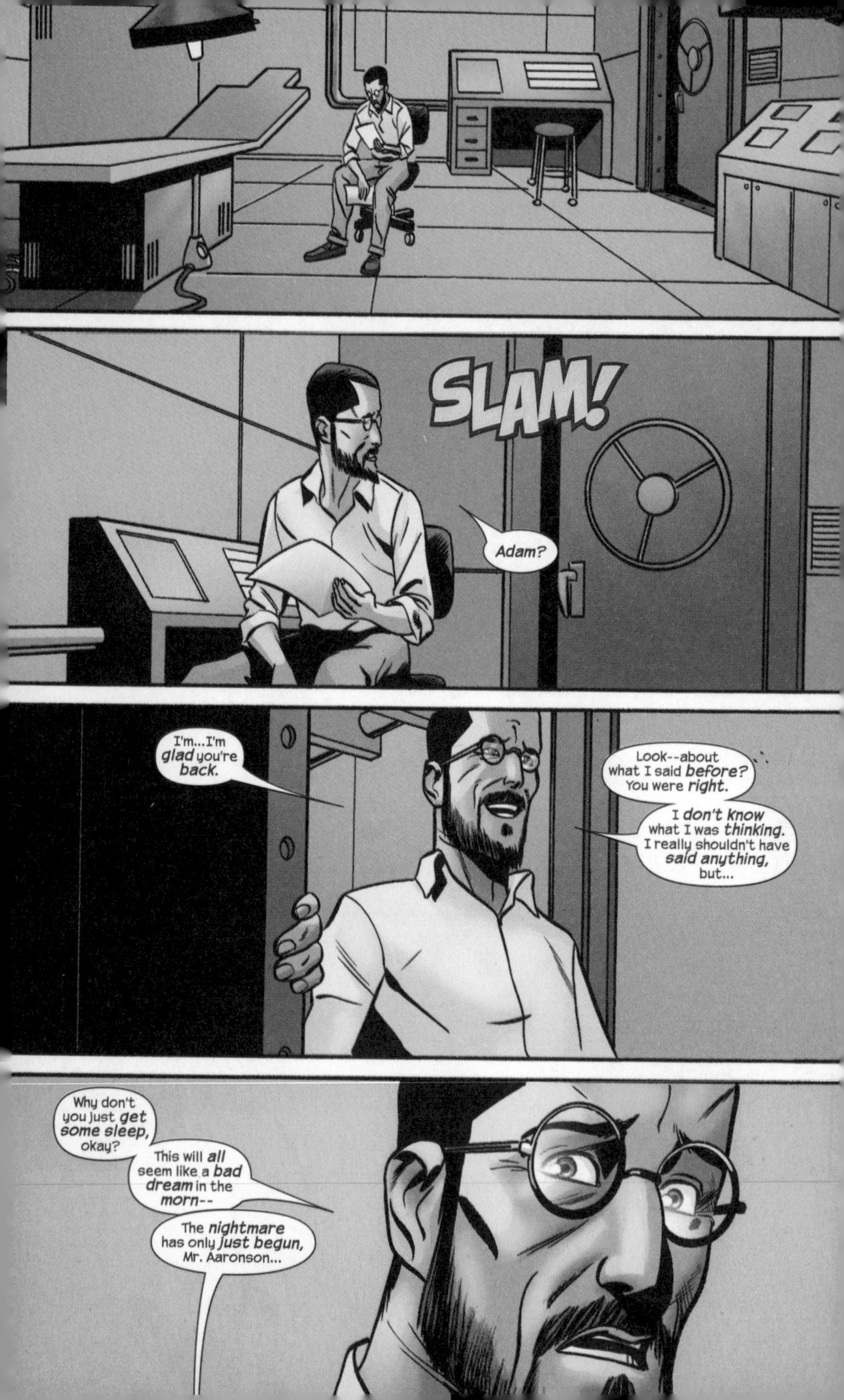
SLAM!
Adam?
I'm...I'm glad you're back.
Look--about what I said before? You were right.
I don't know what I was thinking. I really shouldn't have said anything, but...
Why don't you just get some sleep, okay?
This will all seem like a bad dream in the morn--
The nightmare has only just begun, Mr. Aaronson...

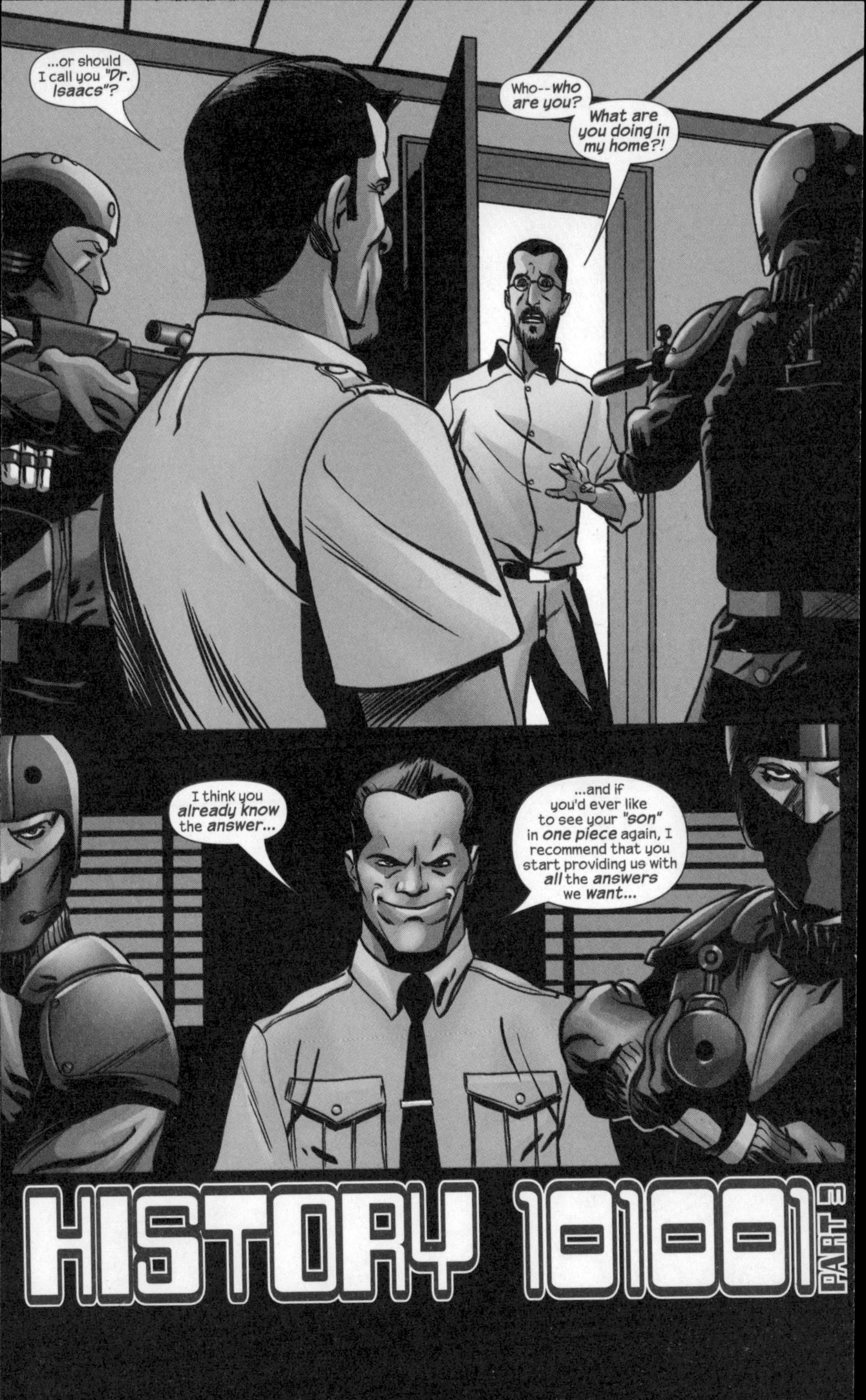
...or should I call you "Dr. Isaacs"?
Who--who are you?
What are you doing in my home?!
I think you already know the answer...
...and if you'd ever like to see your "son" in one piece again, I recommend that you start providing us with all the answers we want...
HISTORY 101001 PART 3

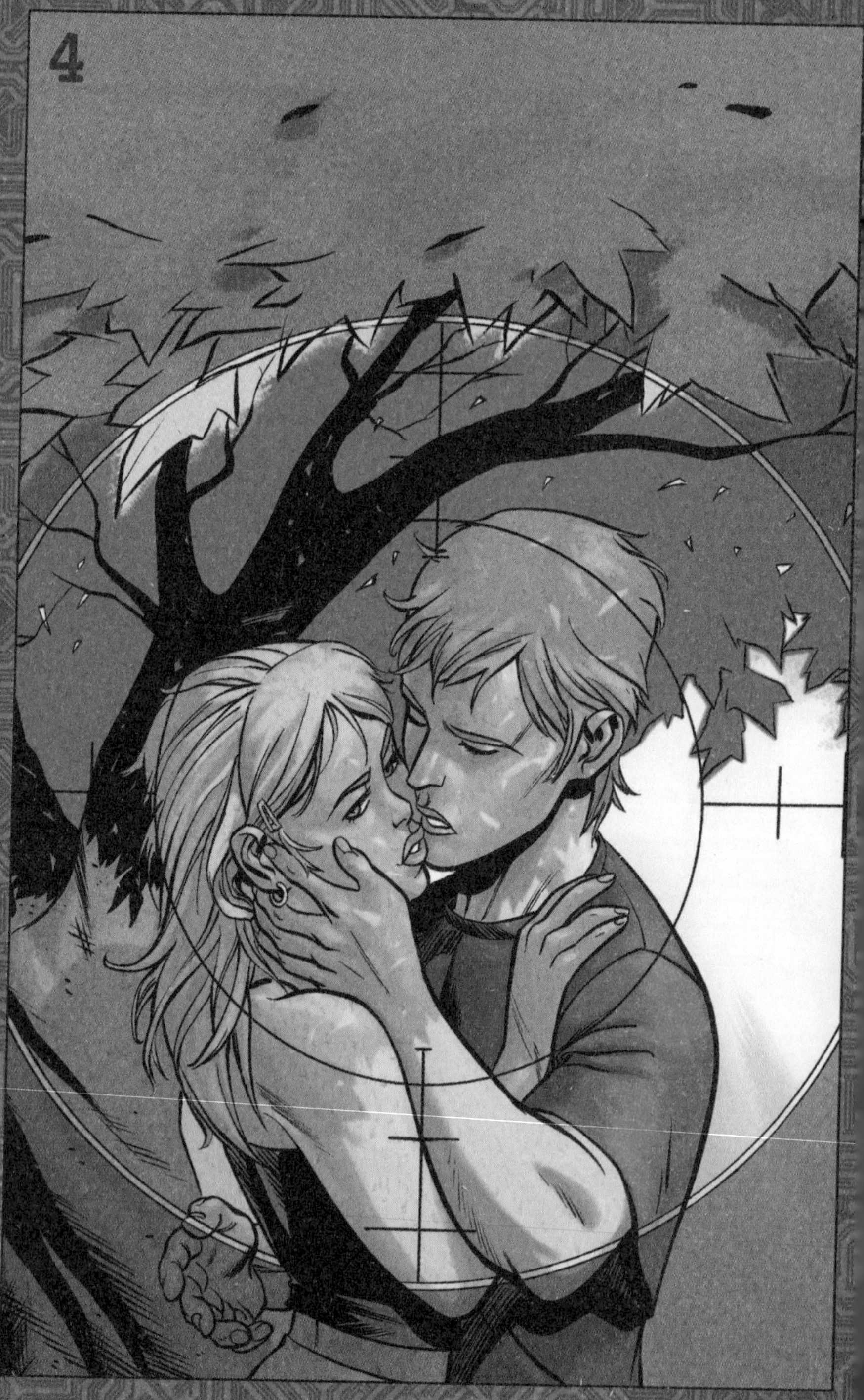
4

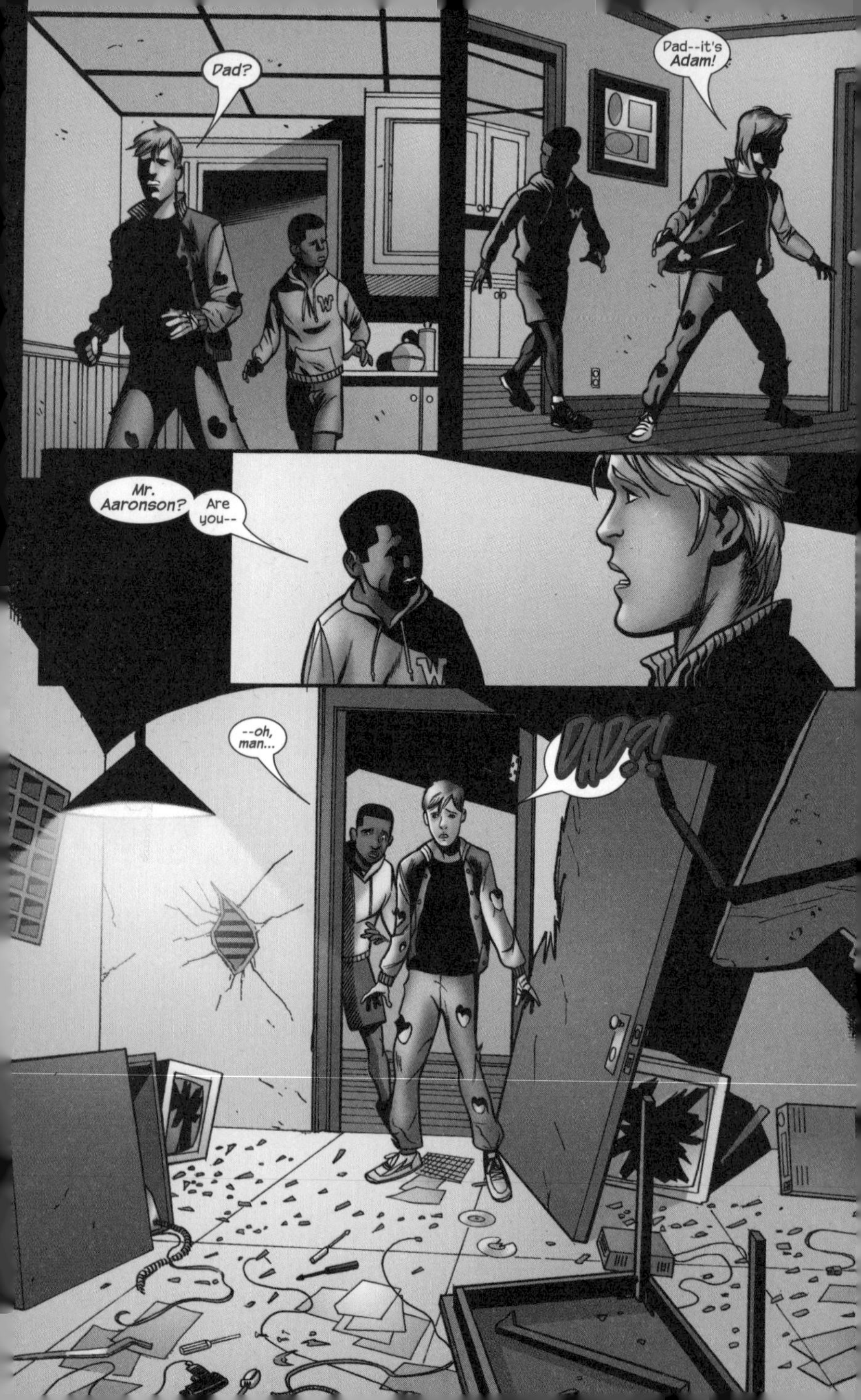
Dad?
Dad--it's Adam!
Mr. Aaronson?
Are you--
--oh, man...
DAD?!

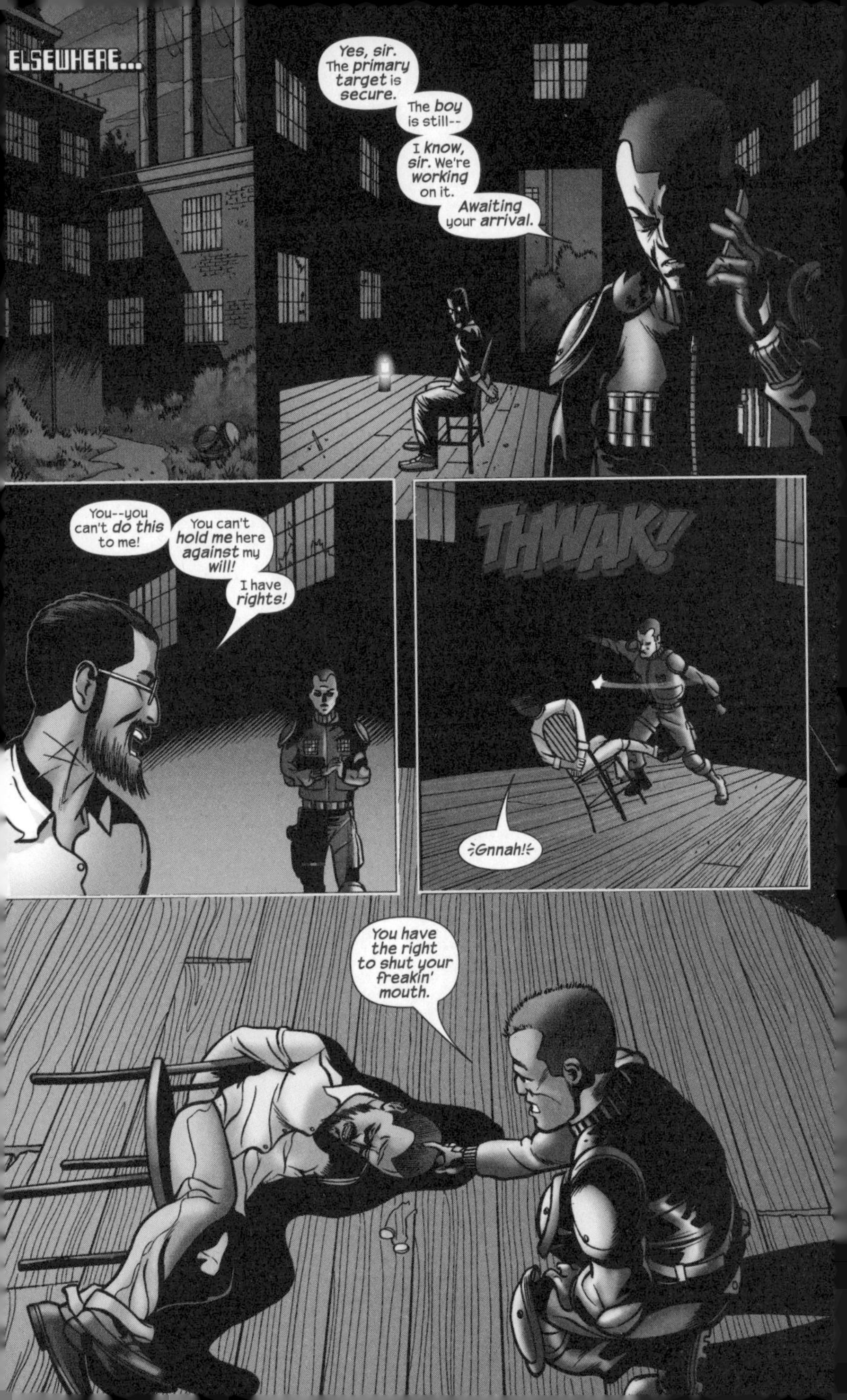
ELSEWHERE...
Yes, sir. The primary target is secure.
The boy is still--
I know, sir. We're working on it.
Awaiting your arrival.
You--you can't do this to me!
You can't hold me here against my will!
I have rights!
THWAK!
Gnnah!
You have the right to shut your freakin' mouth.

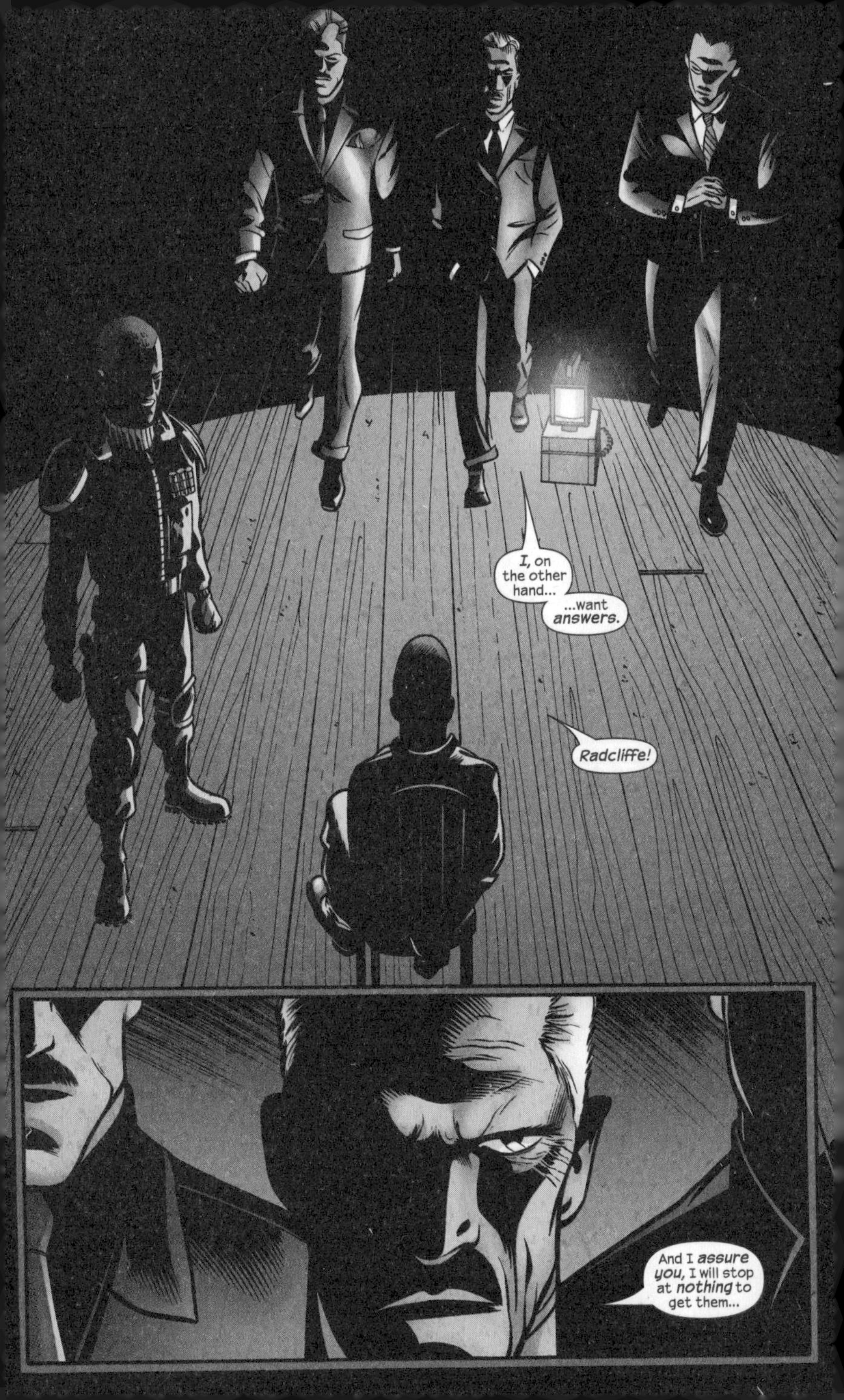
I, on the other hand...
...want answers.
Radcliffe!
And I assure you, I will stop at nothing to get them...

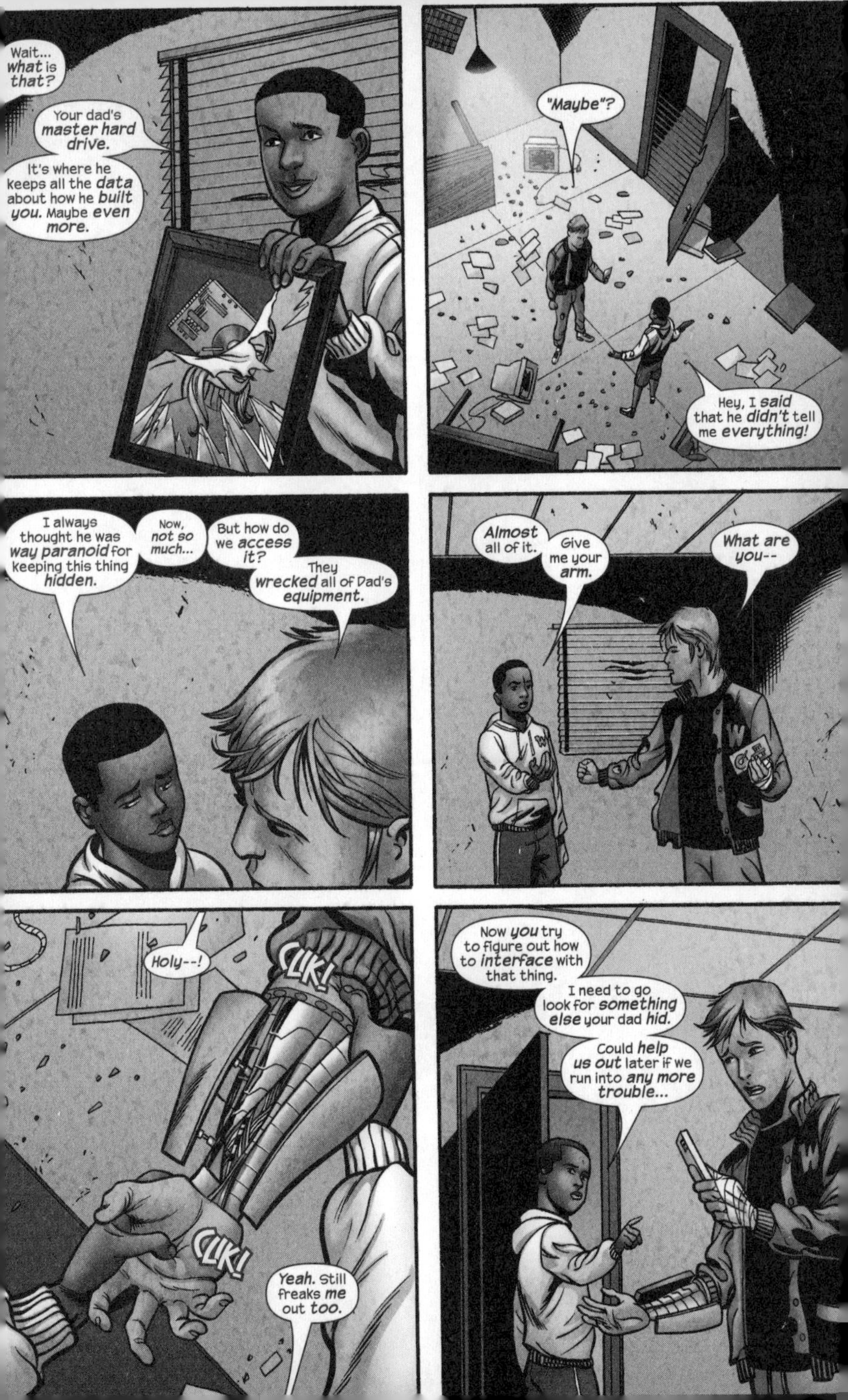

Wait... what is that?
Your dad's master hard drive.
It's where he keeps all the data about how he built you. Maybe even more.
"Maybe"?
Hey, I said that he didn't tell me everything!
I always thought he was way paranoid for keeping this thing hidden.
Now, not so much...
But how do we access it?
They wrecked all of Dad's equipment.
Almost all of it.
Give me your arm.
What are you--
Holy--!
CLIK!
CLIK!
Yeah. Still freaks me out too.
Now you try to figure out how to interface with that thing.
I need to go look for something else your dad hid.
Could help us out later if we run into any more trouble...

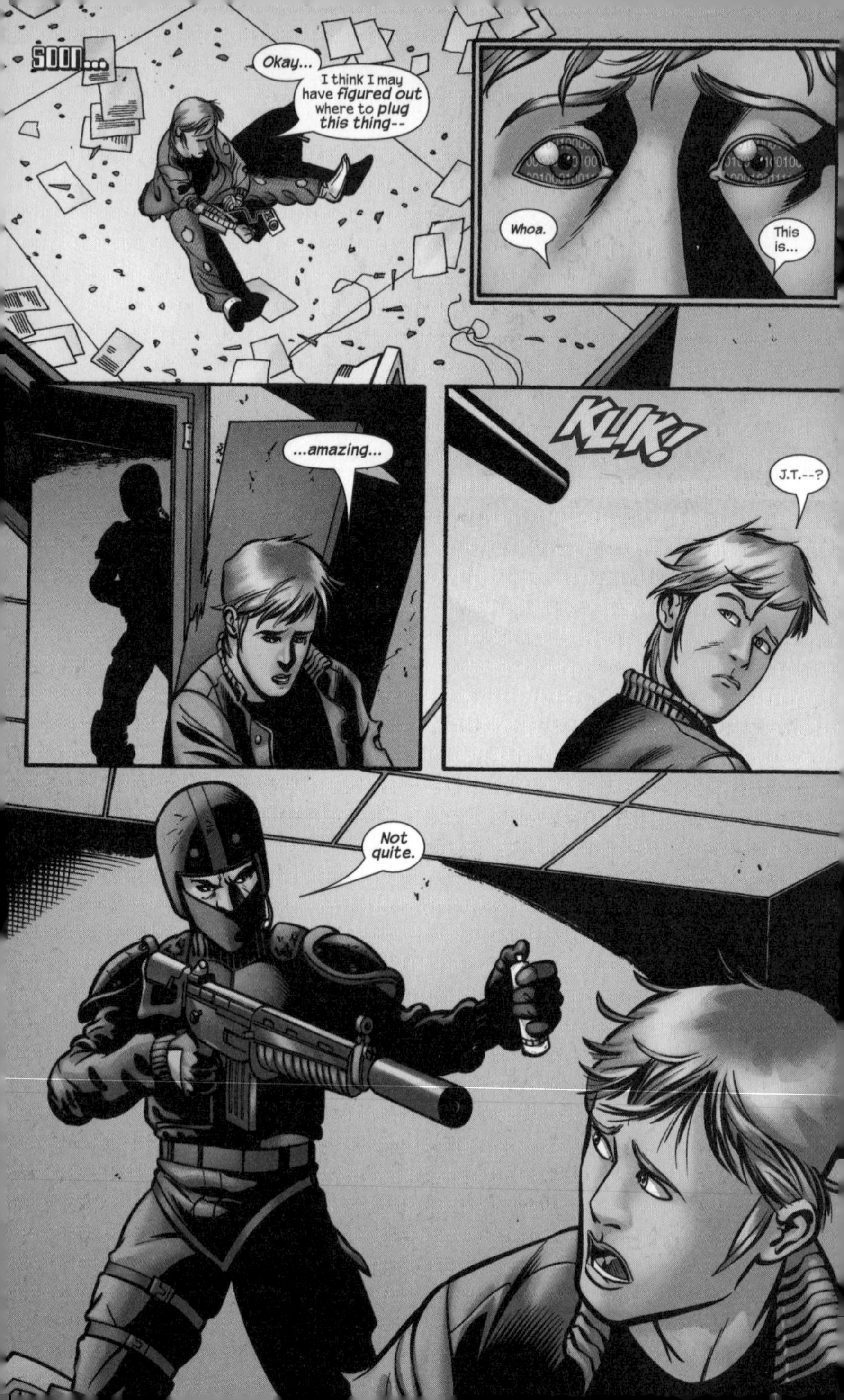
SOON...
Okay...
I think I may have figured out where to plug this thing--
Whoa.
This is...
...amazing...
KLIK!
J.T.--?
Not quite.

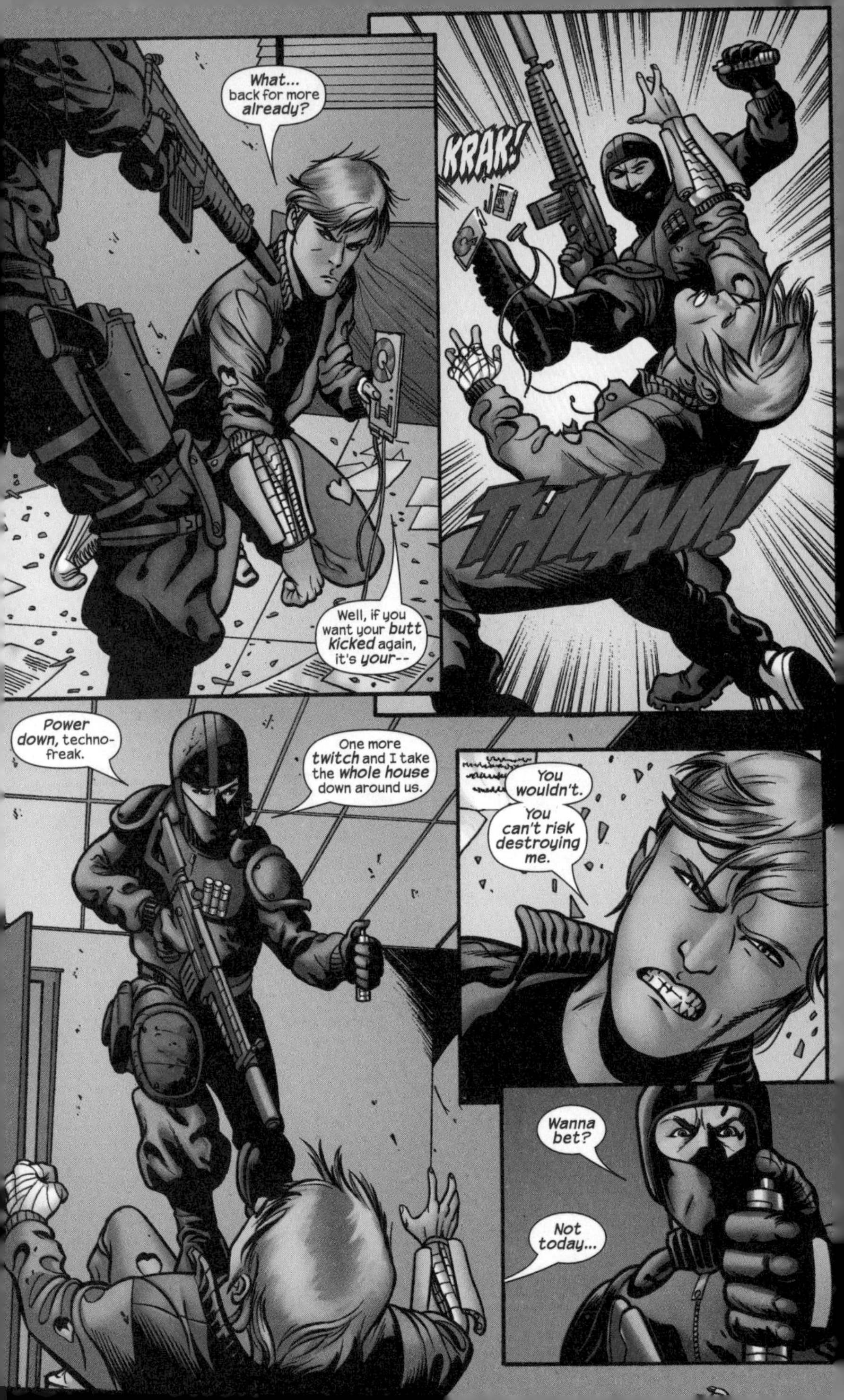
What... back for more already?
Well, if you want your butt kicked again, it's your--
KRAK!
THWAM!
Power down, techno-freak.
One more twitch and I take the whole house down around us.
You wouldn't.
You can't risk destroying me.
Wanna bet?
Not today...

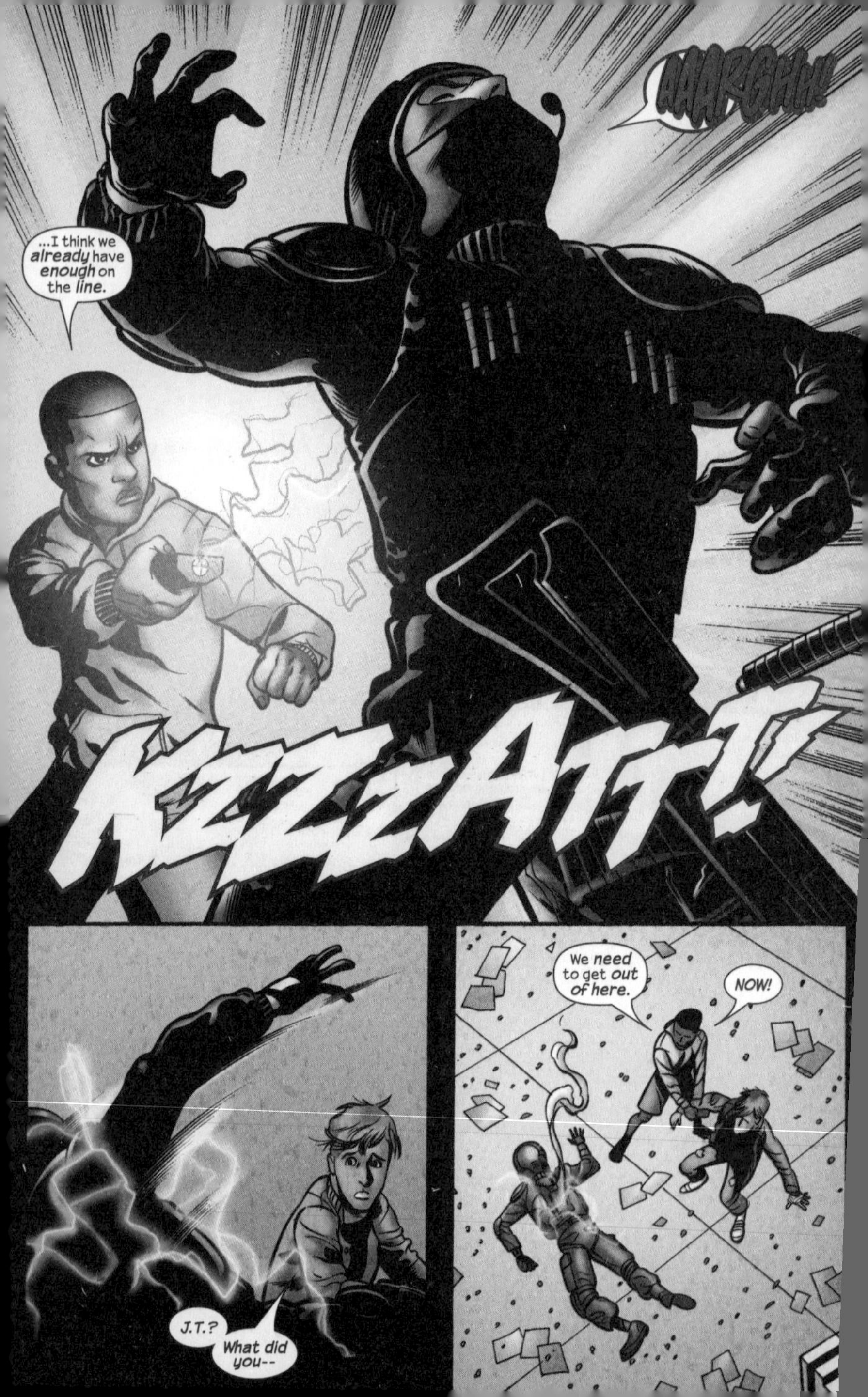

AAARGHHH!
...I think we already have enough on the line.
KZZZATT!
J.T.? What did you--
We need to get out of here.
NOW!

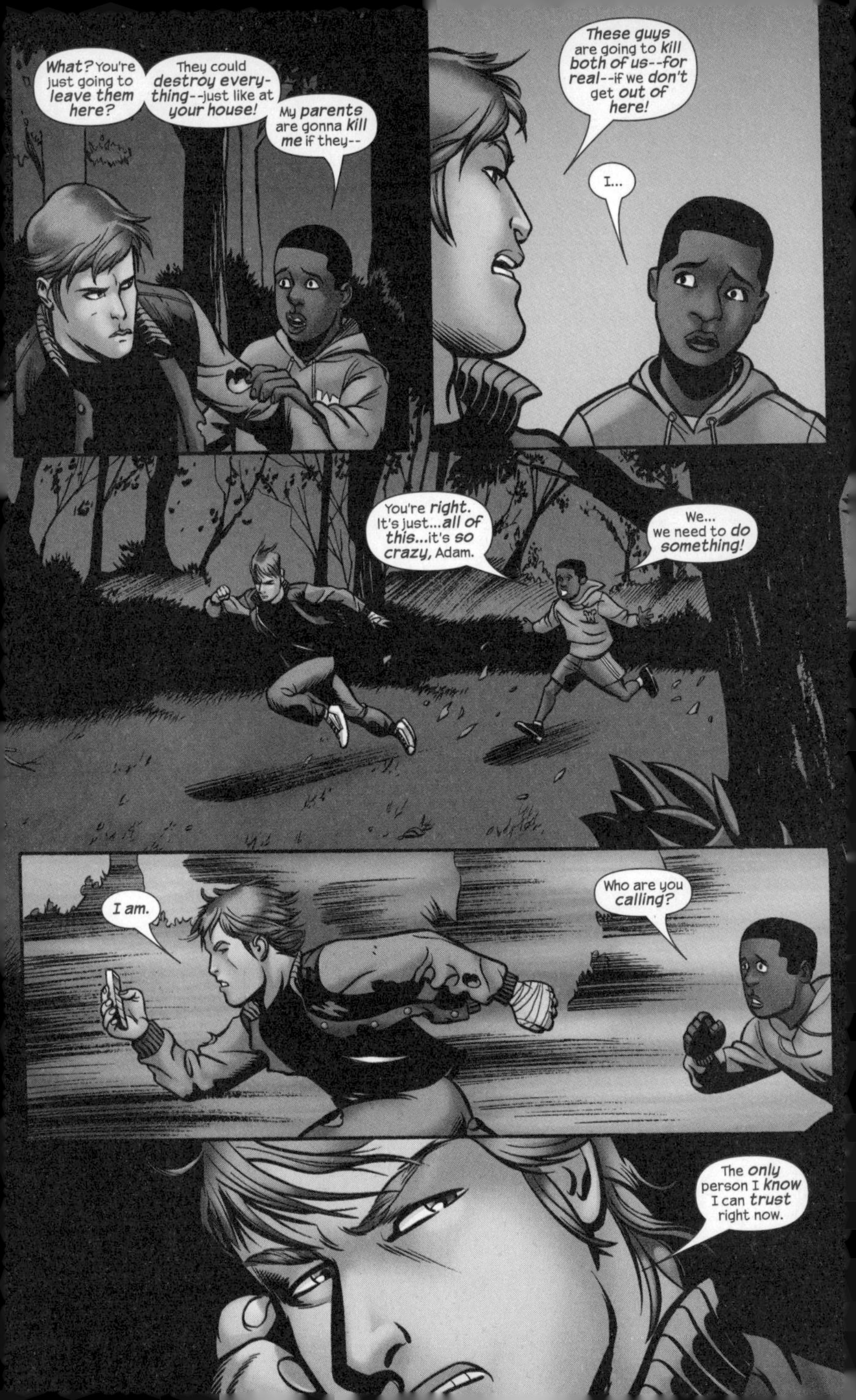
What? You're just going to leave them here?
They could destroy every-thing--just like at your house!
My parents are gonna kill me if they--
These guys are going to kill both of us--for real--if we don't get out of here!
I...
You're right. It's just...all of this...it's so crazy, Adam.
We... we need to do something!
I am.
Who are you calling?
The only person I know I can trust right now.

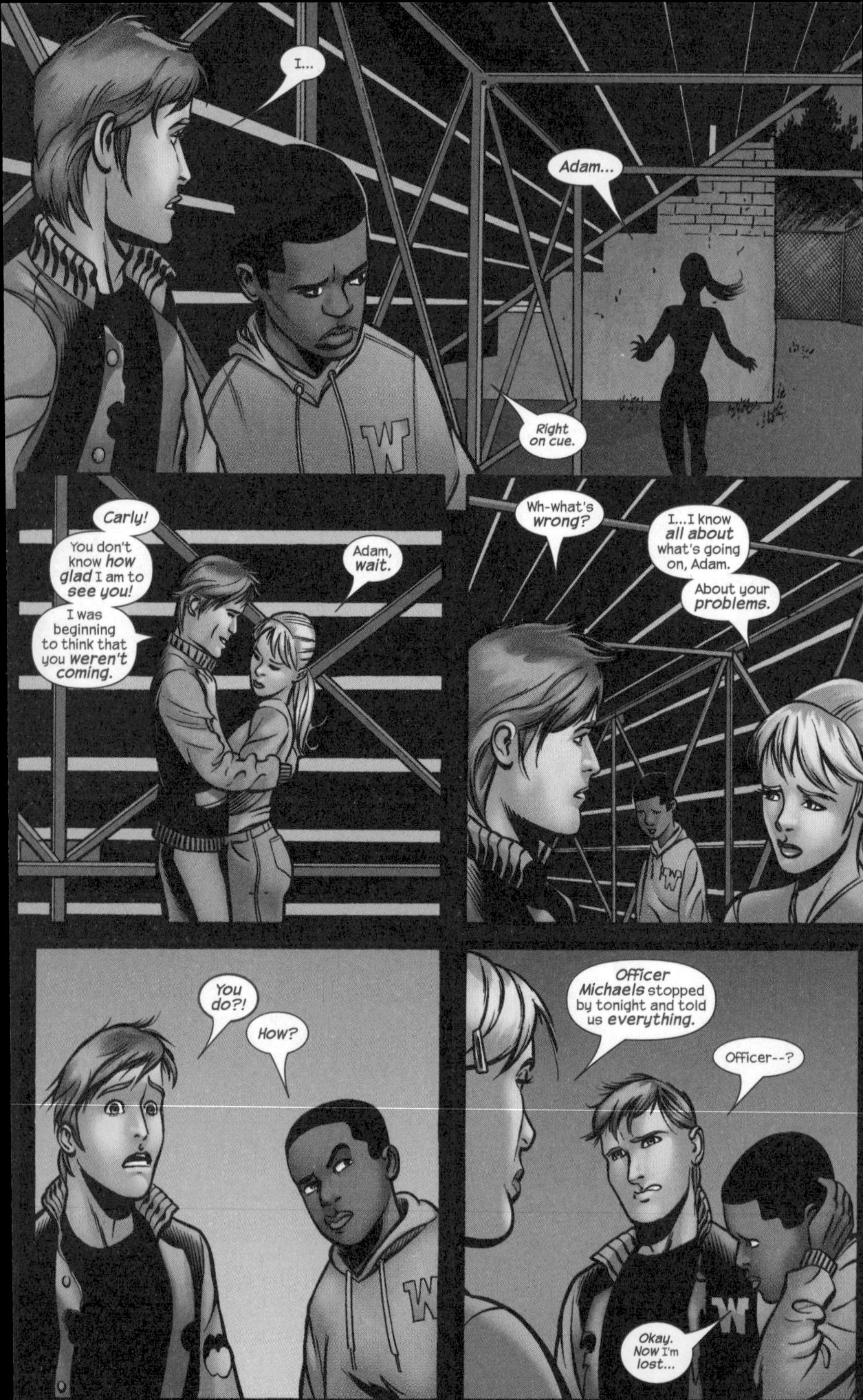
I...
Adam...
Right on cue.
Carly!
You don't know how glad I am to see you!
I was beginning to think that you weren't coming.
Adam, wait.
Wh-what's wrong?
I...I know all about what's going on, Adam.
About your problems.
You do?!
How?
Officer Michaels stopped by tonight and told us everything.
Officer--?
Okay. Now I'm lost...

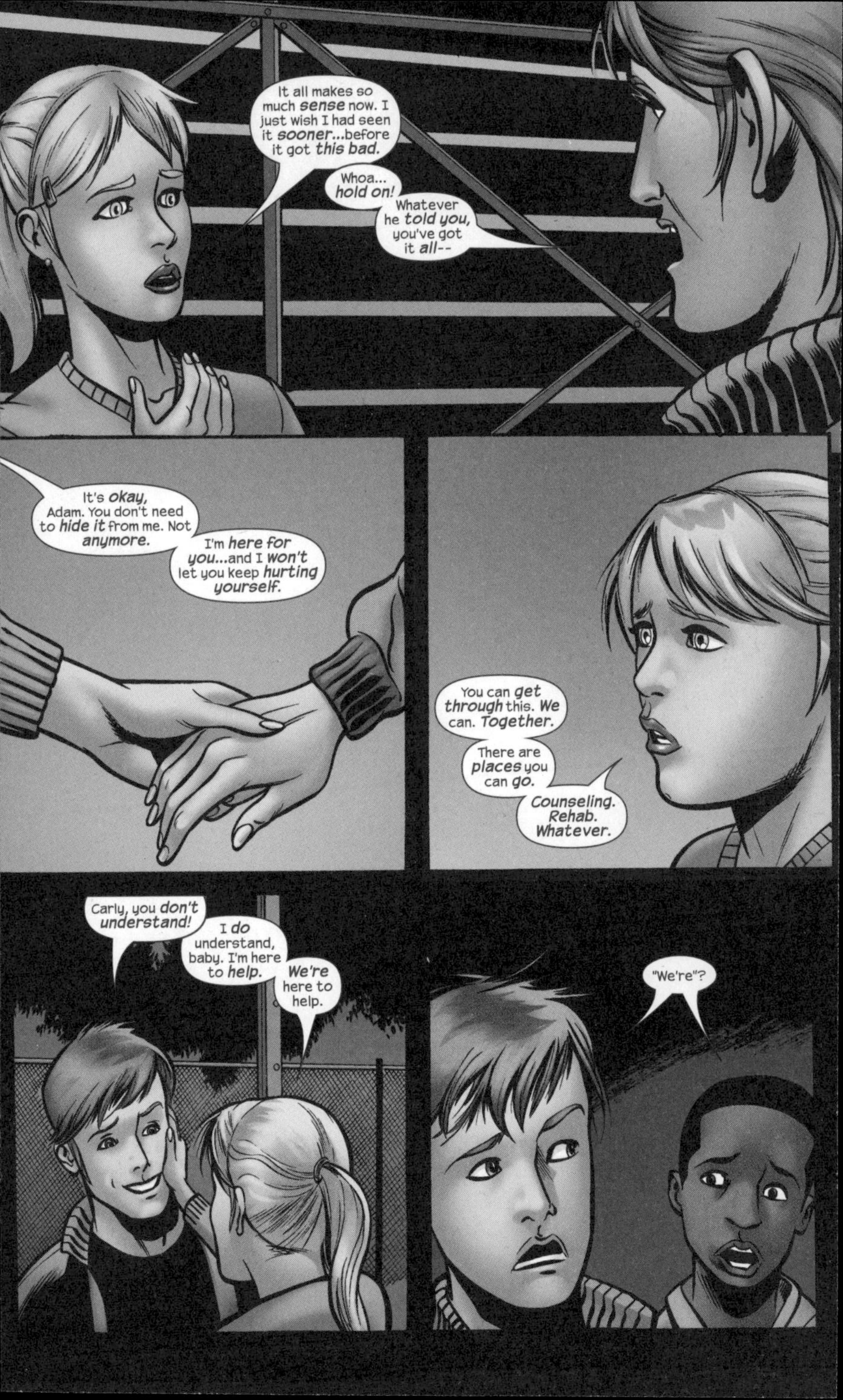
It all makes so much sense now. I just wish I had seen it sooner...before it got this bad.
Whoa... hold on!
Whatever he told you, you've got it all--
It's okay, Adam. You don't need to hide it from me. Not anymore.
I'm here for you...and I won't let you keep hurting yourself.
You can get through this. We can. Together.
There are places you can go.
Counseling. Rehab. Whatever.
Carly, you don't understand!
I do understand, baby. I'm here to help.
We're here to help.
"We're"?

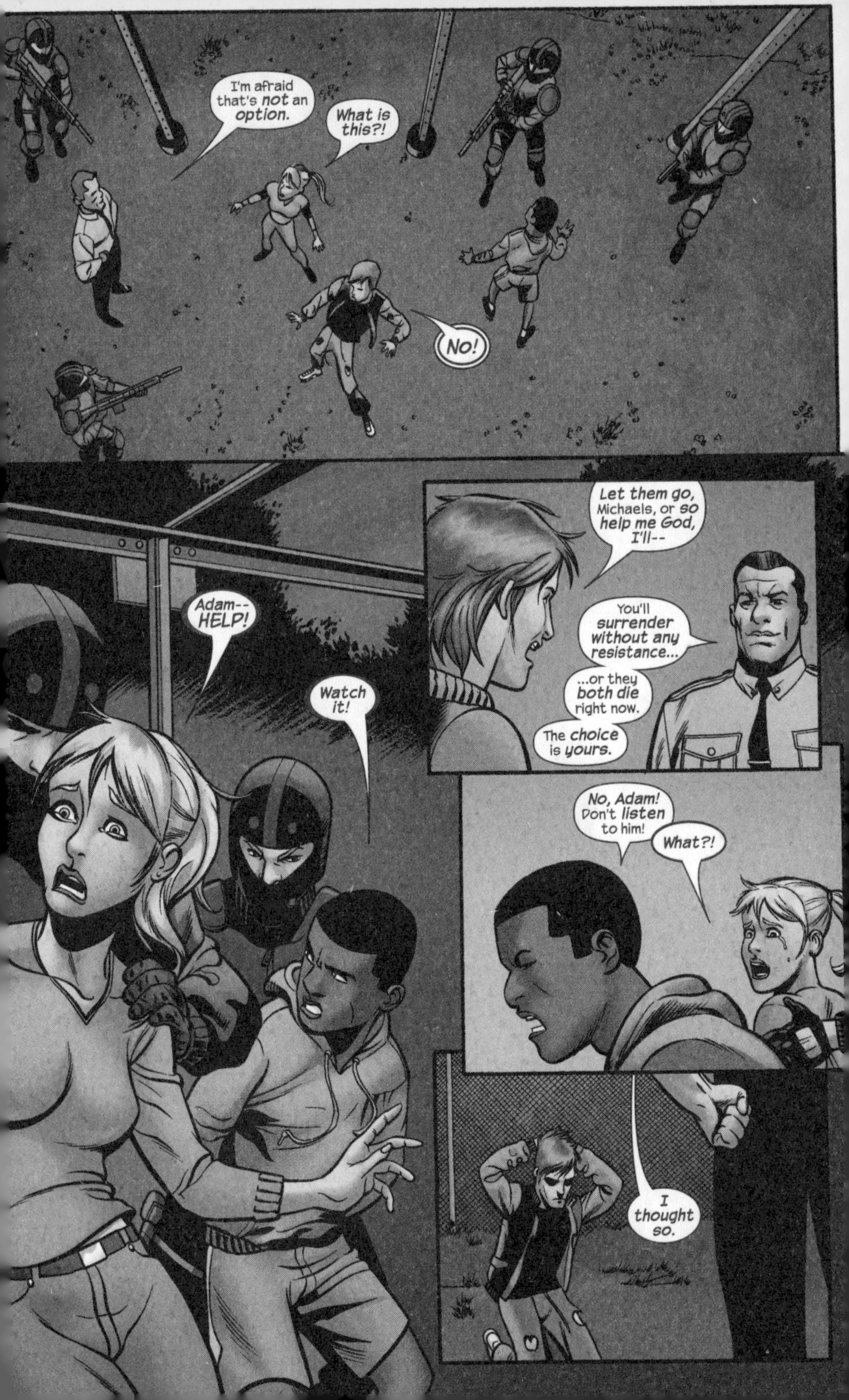
I'm afraid that's not an option.
What is this?!
No!
Adam-- HELP!
Watch it!
Let them go, Michaels, or so help me God, I'll--
You'll surrender without any resistance...
...or they both die right now.
The choice is yours.
No, Adam! Don't listen to him!
What?!
I thought so.

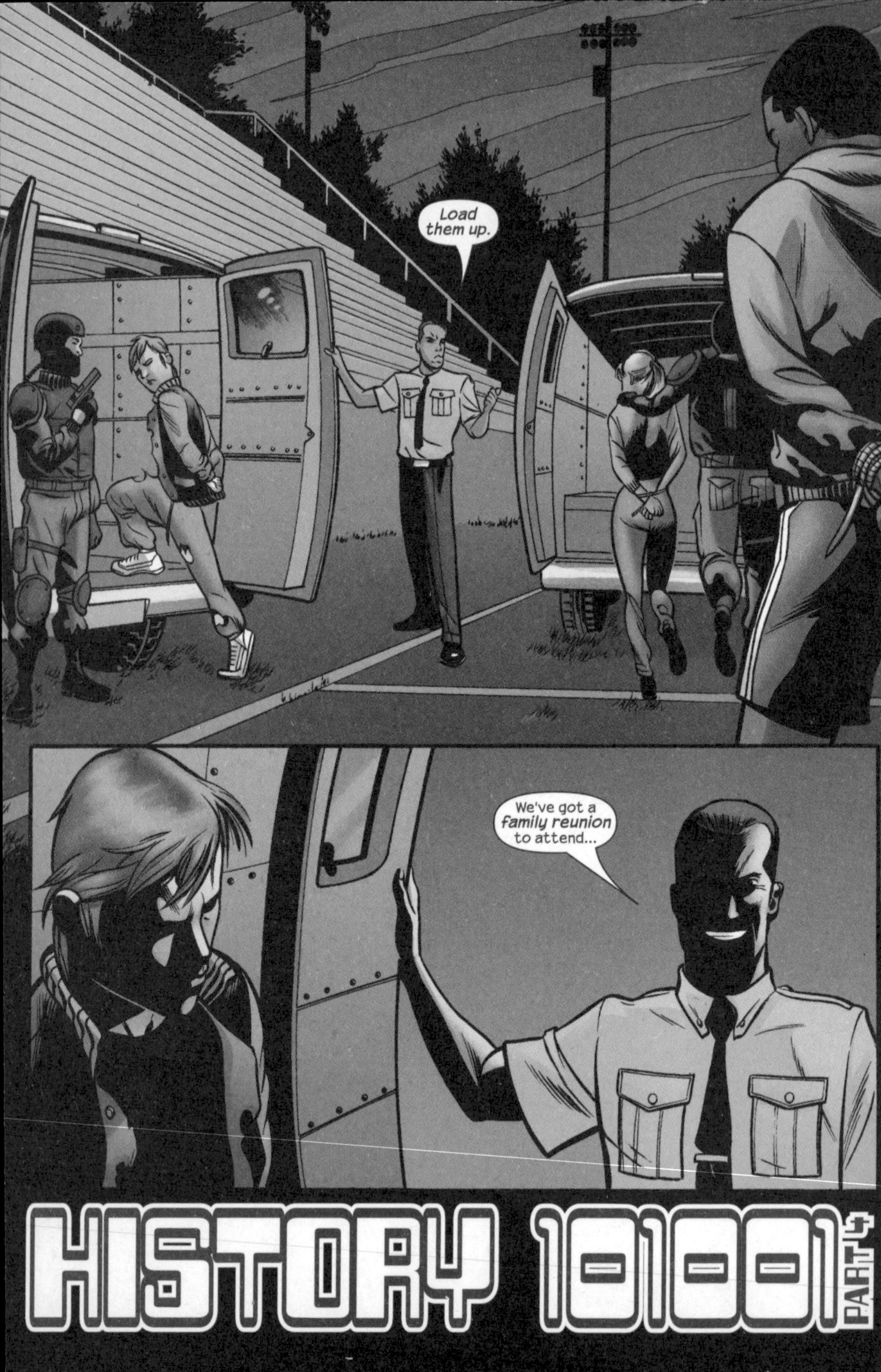
Load them up.
We've got a family reunion to attend...
HISTORY 101001 PART 4

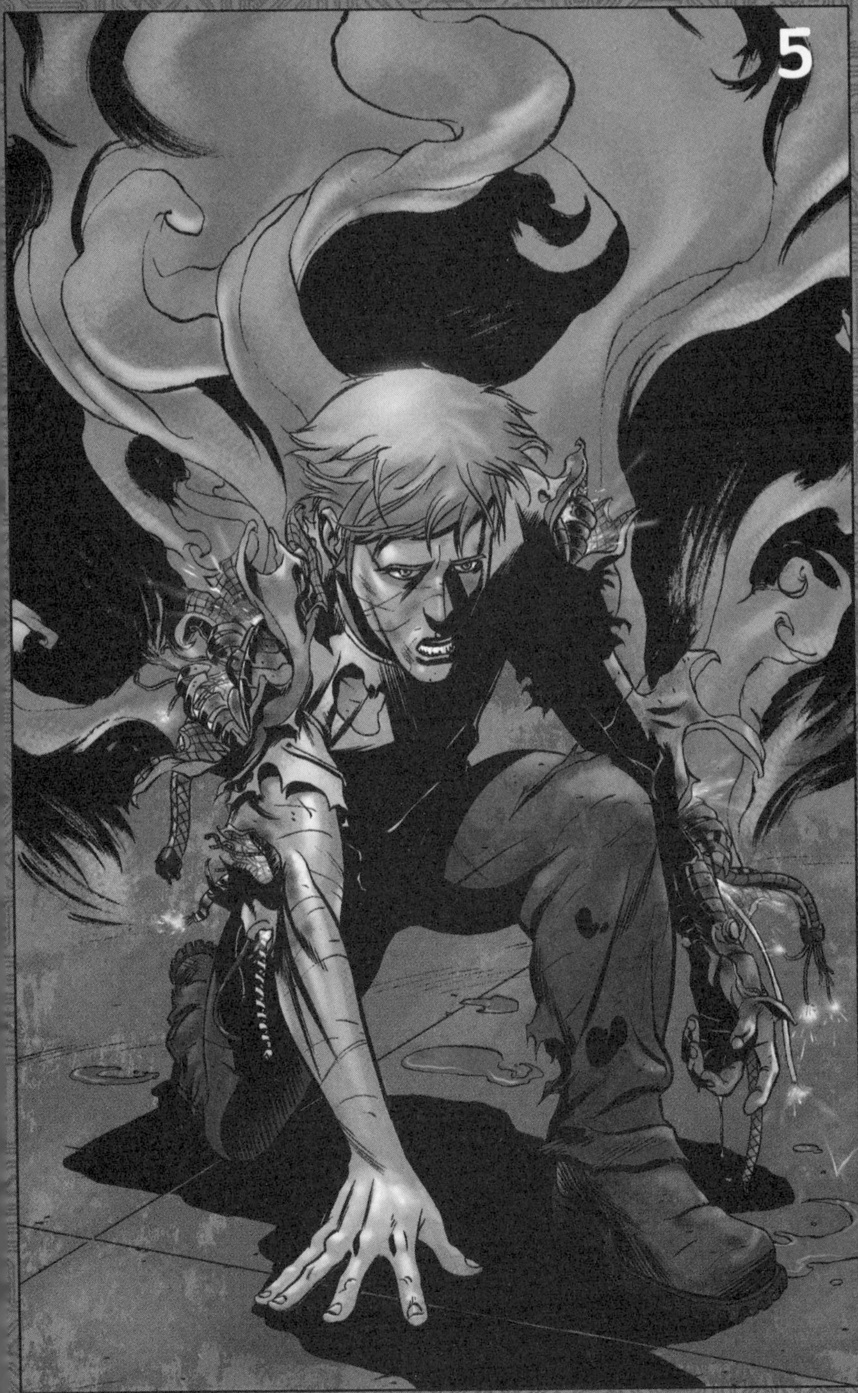
5

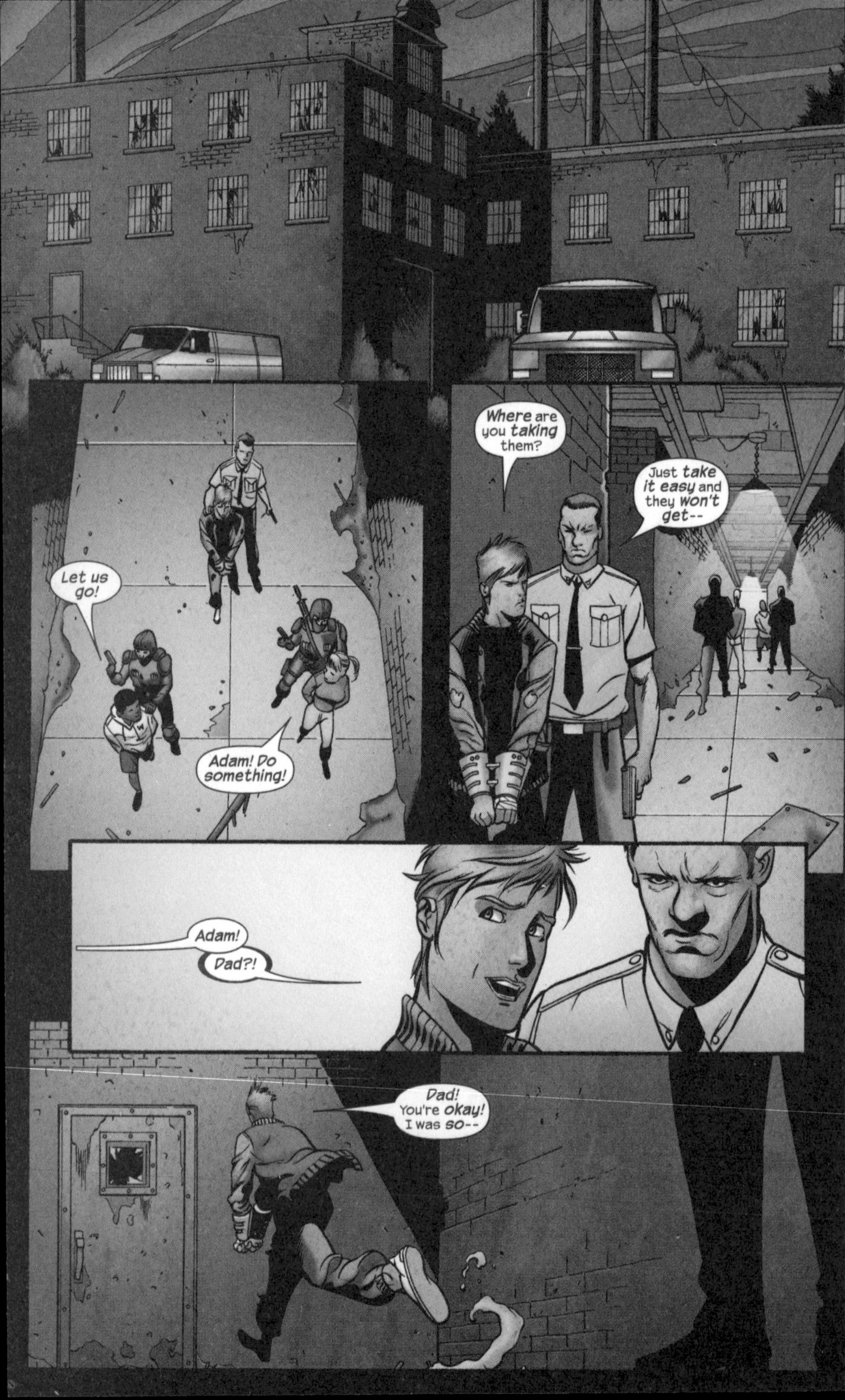
Let us go!
Adam! Do something!
Where are you taking them?
Just take it easy and they won't get--
Adam!
Dad?!
Dad! You're okay! I was so--

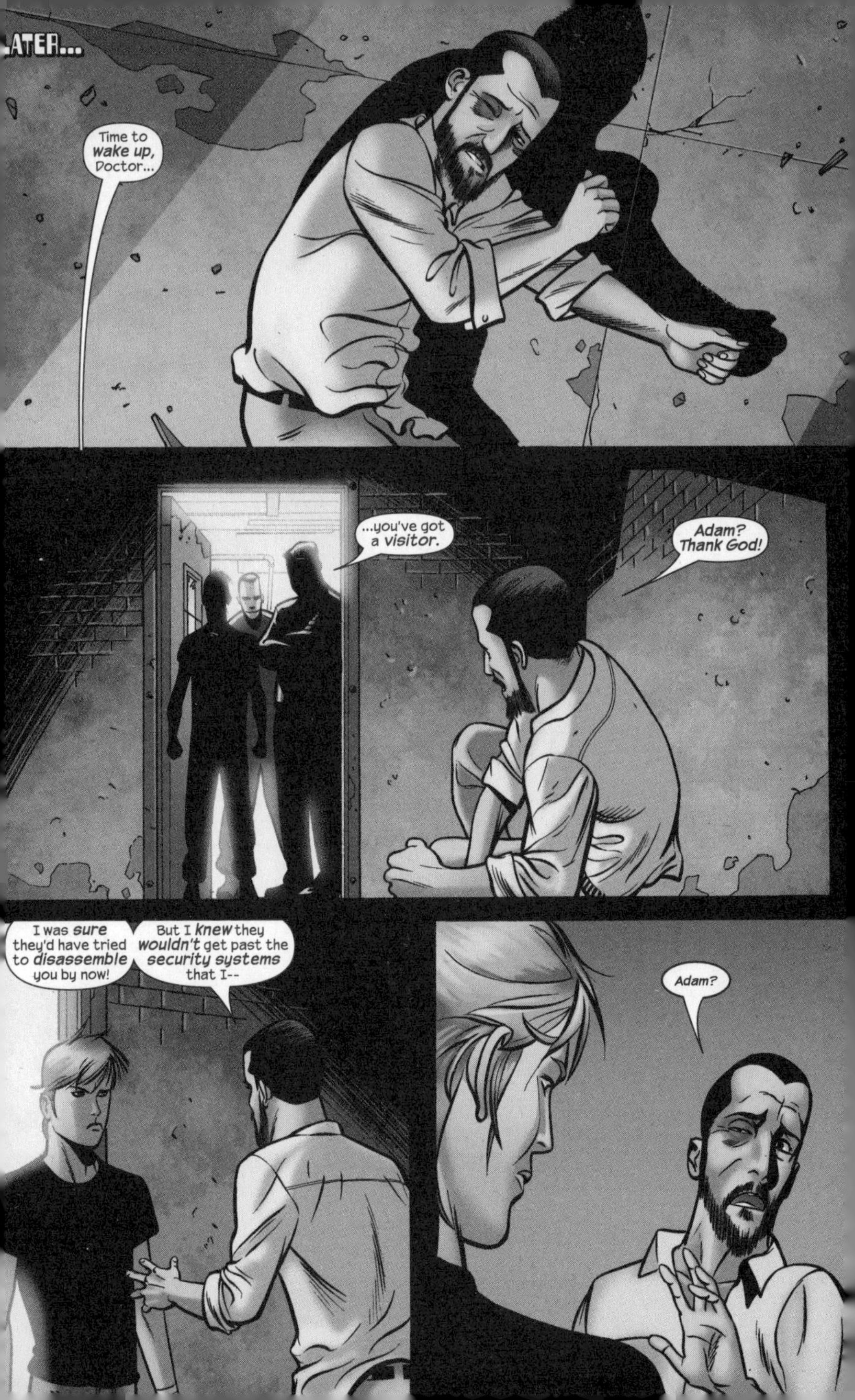
LATER...
Time to wake up, Doctor...
...you've got a visitor.
Adam? Thank God!
I was sure they'd have tried to disassemble you by now!
But I knew they wouldn't get past the security systems that I--
Adam?

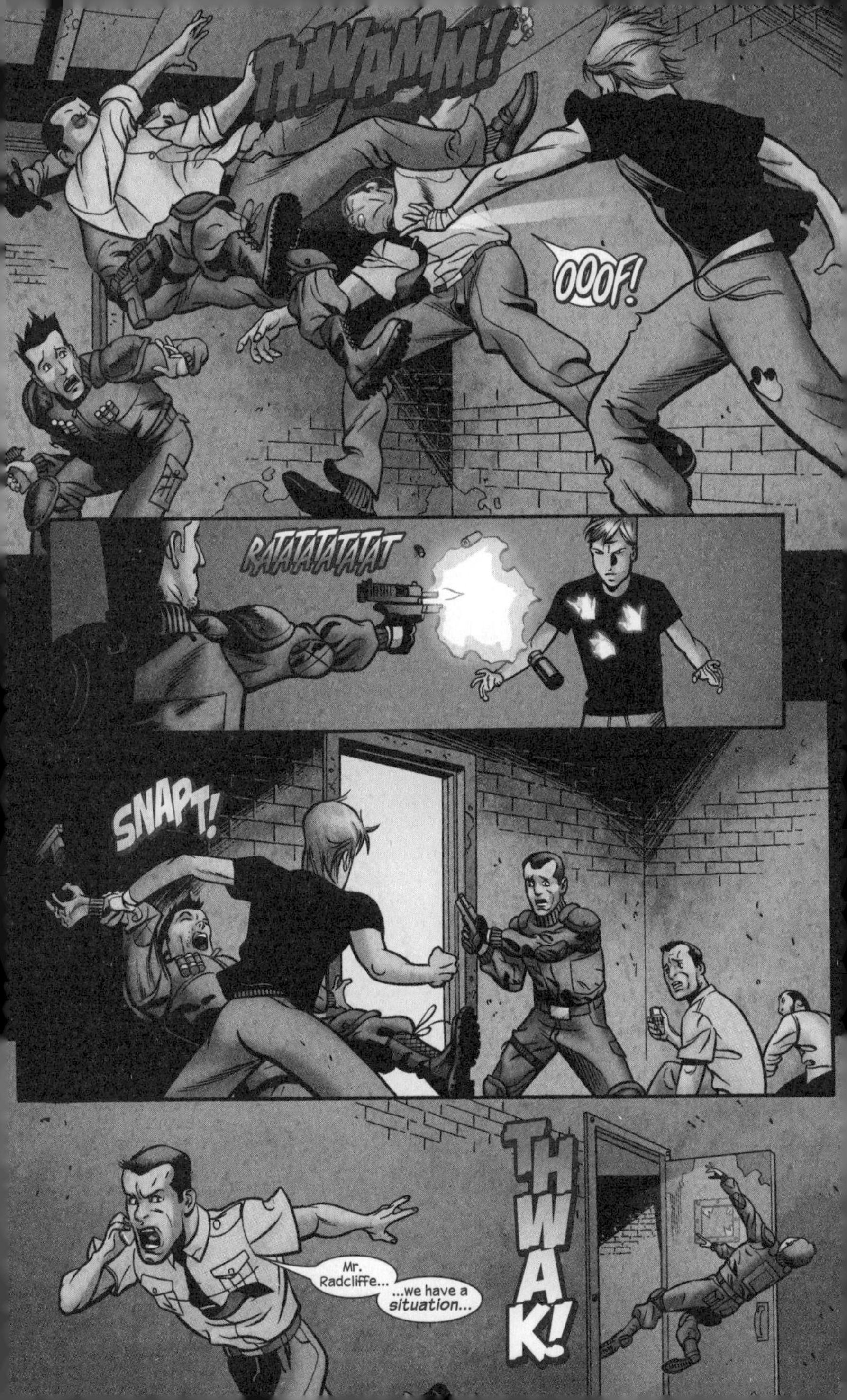
THWAMM!
OOOF!
RATATATATATAT
SNAPT!
Mr. Radcliffe...
...we have a situation...
THWAK!

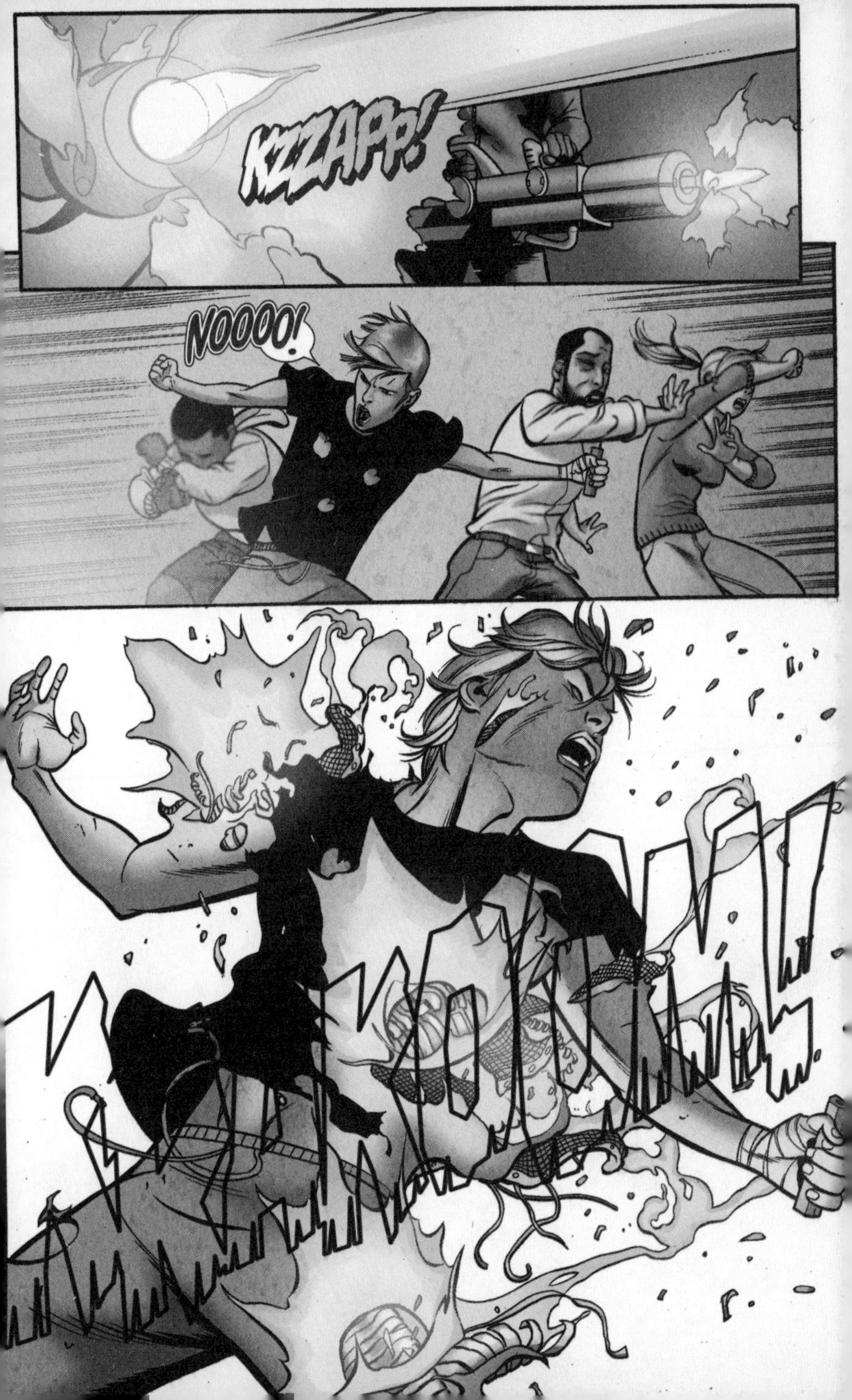
KZZAPP!
NOOOO!

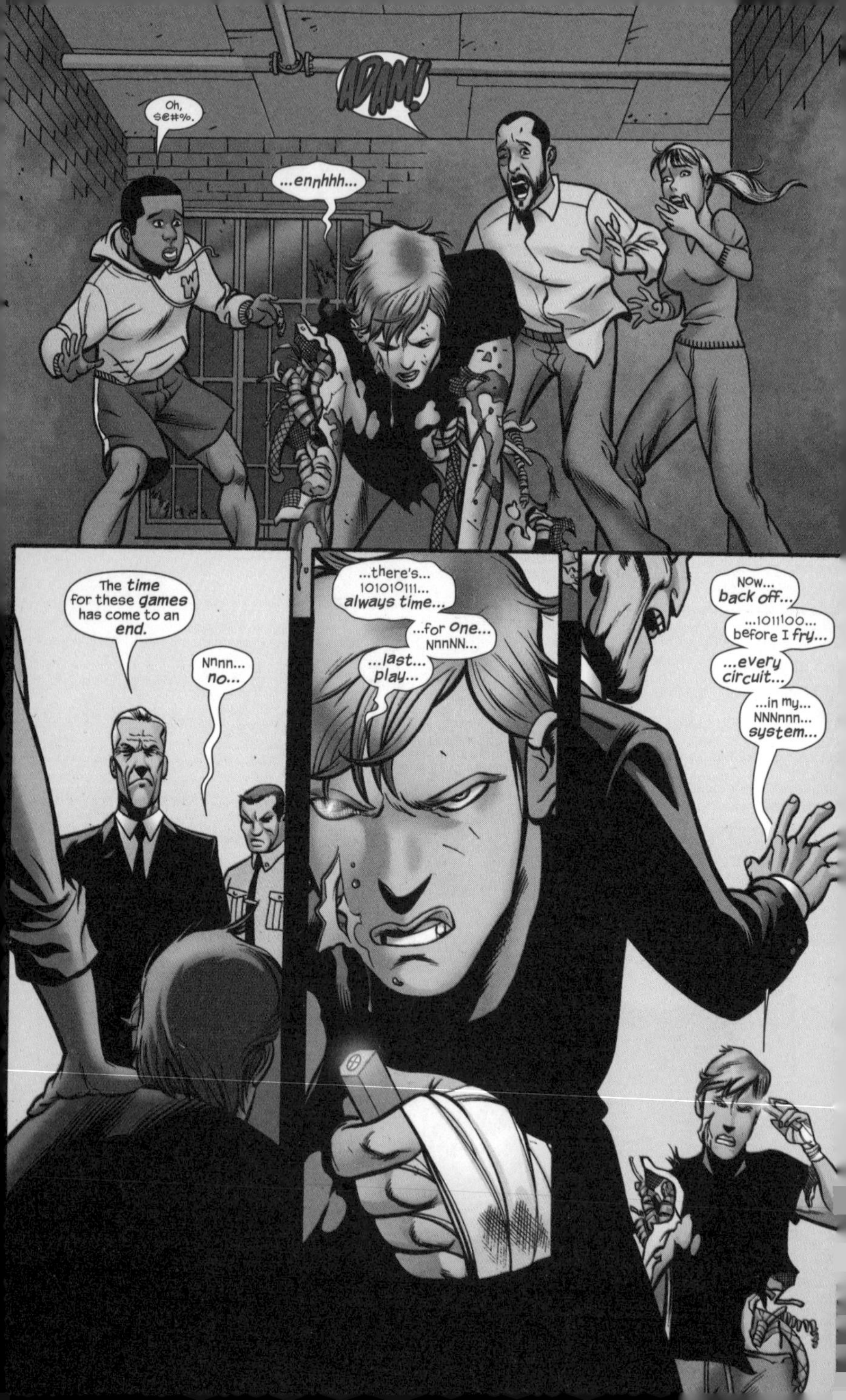
Oh, $@#%.
ADAM!
...ennhhh...
The time for these games has come to an end.
Nnnn... no...
...there's... 101010111... always time...
...for one... NnnNN...
...last... play...
Now... back off...
...1011100... before I fry...
...every circuit...
...in my... NNNnnn... system...

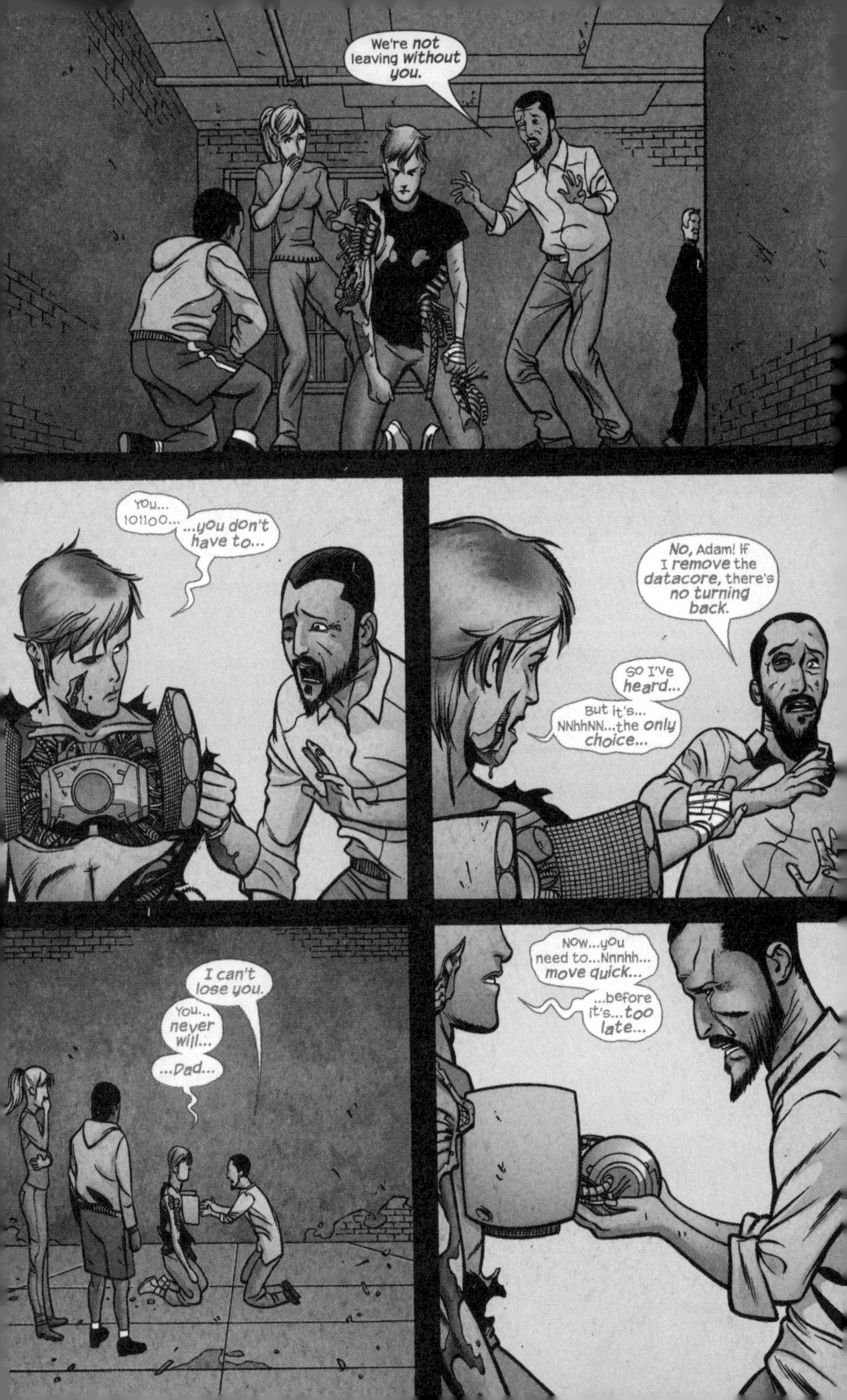
We're not leaving without you.
You... 101100... ...you don't have to...
No, Adam! If I remove the datacore, there's no turning back.
So I've heard...
But it's... NNhhNN...the only choice...
I can't lose you.
You... never will...
...Dad...
Now...you need to...Nnnhh... move quick...
...before it's...too late...

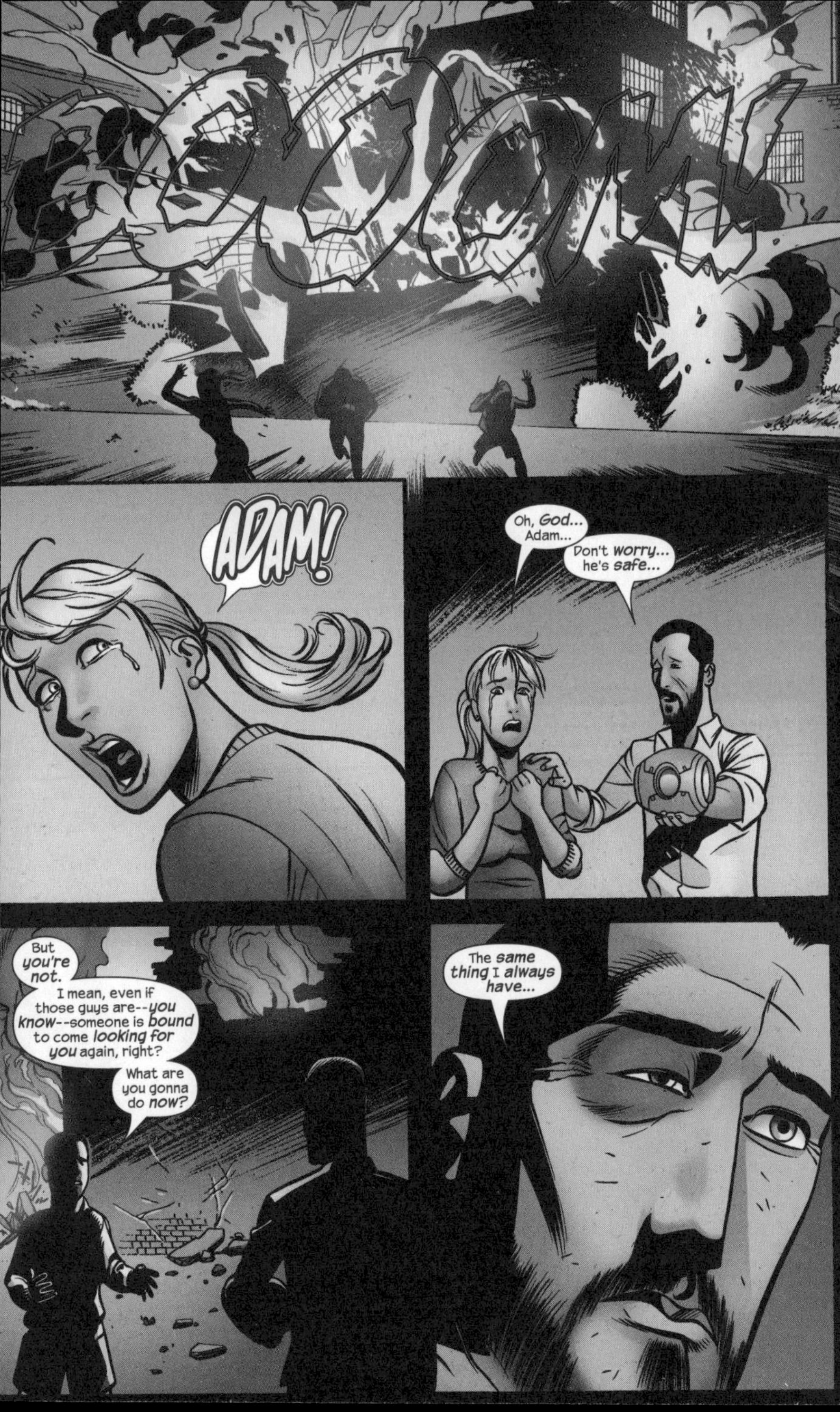
KA-BOOM!
ADAM!
Oh, God... Adam...
Don't worry... he's safe...
But you're not.
I mean, even if those guys are--you know--someone is bound to come looking for you again, right?
What are you gonna do now?
The same thing I always have...

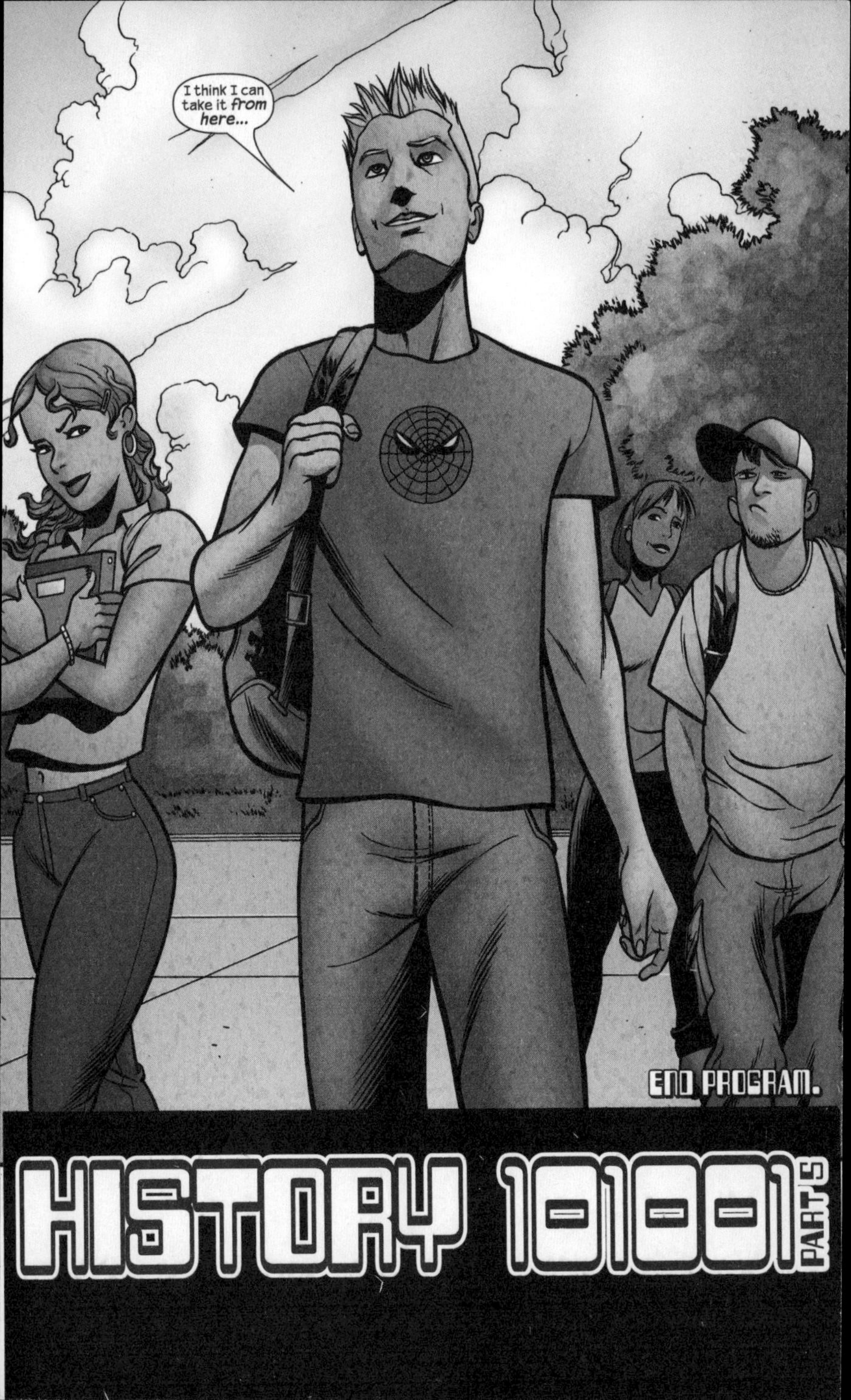
I think I can take it *from* here...
END PROGRAM.
HISTORY 101001 PART 5